© Y. B. Usman

First Published April 1987
1st reprint November 1987
2nd reprint January, 2014

ISBN 978 – 2557 – 08 - 0

Published by the Centre for Democratic Development
Research and Training, Zangon Shanu
P.M.B. 1077, Zaria, Nigeria.

Printed by M. O. Press, Kaduna

"Our state is at the heartland of the northern parts of this country, in every sense of history and culture, economically and politically. But we do not belong to the retrograde north of feudalists, slave-holders, crooks, parasites and foreign agents. We are of the cultured north of democracy, liberation and social progress for all the people of Nigeria".

Alhaji Abdulkadir Balarabe Musa,
Tuesday, 22nd June, 1981.

INTRODUCTION

The meaning and significance of the increasingly violent political campaigns built around religious differences in this country today, can only be fully understood when seen within the larger context of what has been happening to Nigeria, to Nigerians, and to the whole of the African continent over, at least, the last ten years. Central to this larger context are the momentous changes in the objective conditions of life of the majority of Nigerians, and in their perception of the nature and causes of these conditions, their future prospects and possibilities.

Another important element of this larger context is the way the basic economic and social relations at the foundation of the system of the imperialist domination of Africa are increasingly incapable of sustaining this system. These relations now increasingly generate for it ecological, economic, social and political crises, which have worsened over the last decade, and for which it does not seem to have any serious solutions, even of a temporary nature, beyond mere cosmetics.

A third crucial element of this larger context, within which increasingly violent political campaigns built around religious differences occur in this country, is the increasing inability of imperialism and its Zionist, Arab reactionary, and racist South African agents, to subvert, contain, and crush the revolutionary movements and governments which have developed in Africa over the last ten years, and which in spite of savage military attacks and sustained economic offensives have survived various setbacks with an enhanced ideological, political and military capability and cohesion. The decisive

1

advances made over the last decade by the African National Congress of South Africa; SWAPO in Namibia; and by the governments of Mozambique, Zimbabwe, Angola and Ethiopia, in the middle of wars, famines and aggression at all levels, seriously threaten the imperialist order over the whole of Africa more than it has ever been since its establishment several centuries ago.

Within Nigeria, millions of Nigerians are increasingly realising that the present economic and social, system in this country has nothing at all for them and their families', except landlessness, indebtedness, unemployment, destitution, disease, illiteracy and chronic and pervasive insecurity. They are understanding more and more clearly how the vast wealth of their country is being transferred abroad by multinational corporations and banks, who have working for them, in control of the country, a very tiny group of very rich and very unpatriotic Nigerians.

These millions of Nigerians are deeply hostile to the multinationals and detest the role of their Nigerian agents, inside and outside the governments. They increasingly look forward to a fundamental change in the economic and social system to bring to an end the injustices, inequalities, insecurities and indignities daily inflicted on them.

The nation-wide and deeply-felt, popular opposition to the IMF and what it was seen to stand for, which the government tried to channel into a debate in October - December 1985; the recommendations that came out of the Kuru Conference on "Nigerian Foreign Policy to the Year 2000 A.D." of April 1986, which had as participants delegates from national mass and professional organisations and members of the armed forces; the outcome of the political debate of January – September 1986, as conveyed in the report of the Political Bureau, all go to illustrate how this desire for a fundamental change among tens of millions of Nigerians has now come out as a desire for a decisive break away from the path followed by the country in the fast twenty-six years, towards a new path of genuine national independence and socialism.

This momentous change in the outlook and hopes of millions of Nigerians all over the country, is not an accident, an aberration or a bolt from the blue. It arises from concrete processes of change in Nigerian economy and society and in its wider African and world context. The current intensification of political campaigns around religious differences can only be understood within this larger context, and as a continuation of a political pattern which can be clearly traced back to the last years of the Gowon regime when an earlier phase of this process of national radicalisation came to produce Murtala Muhammed and all that he has come to symbolise for millions of Nigerians.

To reduce these violent political campaigns built around religious differences to irrational outbursts by irrational forces is to become a victim of the psychological aspect of the campaign, one of whose purposes is to engender and entrench irrational fears and reflexes so as to block any further advances in the unity of the people of Nigeria, which are necessary if their hopes and aspirations are to be realised.

This collection of essays, letters and documents is intended to be a contribution to the attempt by millions of Nigerians to scientifically comprehend the real issues involved, and to really understand these apparently irrational outbursts threatening their unity, survival and progress. They

3

have been produced over almost a decade, in response to various public issues, and delivered in different forms. Their focus, emphasis and style are therefore not the same. But they all share the common and single purpose of going behind the external appearances, to expose the real nature, and objectives, of the foreign and domestic forces responsible for these increasingly violent political campaigns of religious manipulation in this country. The public documents in the text and in the appendices are intended to illustrate and to provide raw data for the reader to conduct his own assessment and analysis of some of the aspects covered.

In writing the essays and letters in this book, and compiling and publishing it, I have benefitted greatly from working with and having intensive discussions with many people, the contributions of whom are substantial. With some of them we have issued joint statements, two of which are published with other public documents in the appendix. The solidarity and cooperation of all of them is greatly appreciated, even though the responsibility for the contents of this book is entirely mine.

Zaria,
Tuesday, 21st April, 1987.

I. THE MANIPULATION OF RELIGION IN NIGERIA TODAY: ITS SOCIAL AND POLITICAL BASIS*

The subject of this lecture is the manipulation of religion in Nigeria today. What I am going to do is to slightly alter the topic, as advertised, and discuss not so much the social and political context, but the social and political *basis* of this pattern of manipulation.

Definitions

The chairman of the lecture, Patrick Daudu, has in his introduction already started the discussion, which is as it should be. He says that there are various definitions of manipulation and even proposed one within the framework of administrative theory. But since, in the History Department, we have always seen our subject as holistic, dealing with the totality of human existence over time, we take in all the administrative theories and even supersede them!

Now, somebody might ask, why presume that religion is being manipulated in Nigeria today? What is the evidence? Doesn't the very topic of the lecture presume something whose existence has to be established? Something which has to be proved? Is it actually a pattern of manipulation that is unfolding? Or is it merely one of contestation between various religious faiths?

---

*Public Lecture organised by the Students' Union, Institute of Administration, A.B.U., Zaria, Monday, 28th November, 1977. Published in *New Nigerian*, 13th-14th January, 1978, and in *For the Liberation of Nigeria*, New Beacon Books, London, 1979.

It is clearly very important that we are precise about our terms. The key term is manipulation. And in whatever normative context it is placed, *manipulation means, essentially, controlling the action of a person or group without that person or group knowing the goals, purpose and method of that control and without them being aware that a form of control is being exercised on them at all.* On the basis of this definition, what is the evidence that religion is being manipulated, in this country today?

There are some people who would say that all that is happening is a healthy development of people becoming more conscious of their religion, as a way of life, and rejecting secularism. Others would say that what is happening is that 'these Christians' are being put in their place; or that 'these Muslims' are now being dealt with properly, etc. etc. What I want to get across to you is that there is a significant number of influential people, even among you students, who deny that religion is being manipulated to serve particular vested interests, in Nigeria today. It is, therefore, important to establish the pattern of this manipulation before dealing with its basis.

The Assassination of Murtala Muhammed

We could go back into Nigerian history to trace this pattern. But I will start with the developments associated with the assassination of Murtala Muhammed on 13th February 1976, and the consequent investigation, trial and executions. It is a convenient starting-point for brevity and also because of the clarity with which these developments brought *out* the full domestic and foreign dimensions of this pattern of manipulation

On the very day Murtala was assassinated and several days afterwards, it was quite clear that there were domestic and foreign forces operating on this country which tried to present his assassination in religious terms in order to foster communal violence. The domestic forces were made up of two main tendencies. There were those that wanted to present Murtala as a Muslim martyr and his assassins as Christian villains. Then there were those that wanted to present Murtala as a Muslim villain and his assassins as Christian redeemers. The foreign dimension manifested itself very clearly in the dispatch from Reuters sent by their chief Nigerian correspondent, Colin Fox, and broadcast over the British Broadcasting Corporation, which said that communal violence had broken out over Murtala's death in parts of the country. Coordinated with all these, at the public level, was a so-called message of condolence from an evangelical organ- isation controlled by a foreign government, 'to Nigerian Muslims for the loss of a Muslim leader'. This message came a few days late to have the intended effect. In any case the powerful, popular and national response, unprecedented in our history, made such machinations much more difficult.

A significant characteristic of all these forces, domestic and foreign, was that they were all bitterly opposed to the domestic and foreign policies of the government under Murtala. The domestic forces were all, almost openly, opposed to the decision on the ex-governors announced by Murtala in his broadcast of 3rd February 1976. Usman Faruk, Joseph Gomwalk and Abba Kyari, for example, were presented as religiously devout leaders most unfairly treated. The foreign forces from Britain, America and Saudi Arabia were bitterly opposed to the patriotic and decisive policies on

7

Southern Africa, especially support for the M.P.L.A., which not only America and Britain were fiercely opposing but even the Saudi government was opposing by funding F.N.L.A. The point I want to get across is that all these forces were jointly and bitterly opposed to Murtala. But the moment he was assassinated these same divisive forces took what would appear as diametrically opposed stands, on ostensibly religious grounds. The fact that all of them were fundamentally hostile to the new direction, towards genuine independence and national cohesion and common purpose, the country was taking, and all of them said Murtala was turning Nigeria to communism, was camouflaged under a fake rivalry.

This particular episode of the manipulation of religion did not stop with the immediate aftermath of the assassination. Attempts seem to have been made to hamper the investigations, trial and executions of those who conspired to assassinate Murtala by spreading what is now becoming a standard tool - religious blackmail. Fortunately the government did not succumb to this.

Chike Obi, the *Drum* and the *New Breed*

The second significant, public manifestation of this pattern of manipulation was connected with a speech by Chike Obi at the 1976 National Union of Nigerian Students' (N.U.N.S.) Convention at Enugu. In this speech Chike Obi isolated Islam and the Fulani for a special attack as factors causing backwardness. If the speech had remained as a speech at a convention it perhaps would not have had the national significance it came to have.

8

But clearly this was not just a speech at a convention. The Department of History at this university was specially invited to write a rejoinder to it by the editors of the *Drum* magazine, with an implicit offer of remuneration. Our reply was that since there is a Department of History at the University of Lagos, where Obi teaches Mathematics and at other universities closer to Lagos, why send all the way to Zaria for a rejoinder on what is made to seem an historical issue? We asked, was this invitation sent to us in order to generate a sensational controversy, which an attack, from a department in Ahmadu Bello University on Chike Obi's statements on Islam and the Fulani, could be used to create? 1 knew *Drum's* South African roots and I noticed on the letter head that Chief Rotimi Williams was one of its directors, so I added something about their desire to make profits at whatever expense to our country. *Drum*, for some reason, did not carry the speech.

But Chike Obi's speech did appear in *New Breed* another journal with an equally dubious purpose. The publication of that speech produced violent reaction and counter-reaction across the country and the government tried to seize some of the copies of that edition. The responses, I think, were quite expected and suited this style of manipulating religion, especially as it is spiced with crude ethnic chauvinism by Chike Obi. This whole episode was a typical exercise in provocation deliberately intended to produce violent reactions and equally violent counter-reactions. It is an example of a well-tuned act of manipulating religion in Nigeria today.

The So-called 'Sharia Debate'

The third significant public manifestation of this pattern of manipulation continued to have the characteristics of provocation – reaction – counter-reaction, through the agency of the mass media. Most of this has had as its excuse what is called 'the Sharia Debate'. But there was one important episode which did not have this excuse, but clearly was part of the pattern. This was the article in the *Sunday Times*, which appeared just before the Festac Durbar. This article took on a tone of hostile and insidious references to both Islam and Christianity. The federal government issued a warning on this but this warning, although in strong language, was ignored as the so-called 'Sharia Debate' was deliberately pushed to become the most prominent issue in the discussion of the future constitution. This 'debate' provided an excuse for the publication of provocative and scurrilous articles purporting to oppose or support the Sharia in newspapers, especially the *Punch*, the *NewNigerian* and the *Nigerian Standard*. The media also amplified various statements and communiqués from symposia and seminars organised ostensibly to debate the constitution, but actually as part of this campaign of provocation – reaction – counter-reaction, the main feature of this phase of the pattern of manipulation.

The Constituent Assembly provided another forum for this campaign to be continued, even more stridently. The rehearsals for this had been started in the Constitution Drafting Committee. The element of numbers is brought in here more clearly tying in the manipulation of religion with the manipulation of ethnicity, statism and regionalism, quite conveniently.

But at the assembly, just as at the seminars, symposia and in the media, there was really no debate in the sense of an articulation and consideration of basic issues and dimensions of the matter. There were statements and counter-statements made up of a series of assertions of strength, threats of civil war and bloodshed and then pious pleas for unity; and then the same cycle of assertions, threats and pleas is repeated again. The very obvious fact that the whole judicial system of the country is stacked against the common people finds no place in this sordid circle of non-debate intended primarily to create a religious and ethnic constituency framework for self-aggrandisement, it is a well-known fact that the peasants and workers of this country – the true and only majority in numbers and production, and the true and only minority in power and wealth – avoid contact with the police and the judiciary because they fear the harassment, intimidation and swindling that usually follows. It is well known that the bourgeoisie have no such fear and some of them even boast of what they can do. It is well known that this is one of the fundamental causes of insecurity and crime. And only a police and judicial system serving the masses and rooted in their midst can deal with this, whatever the law is. All these well-known facts are barely mentioned in the current campaign of provocation – reaction – counter-reaction, which we are supposed to believe is about the future judicial system for the people of this country!

The Standard Explanations for this Pattern
But having established an outline of the public mani-festations of this pattern of manipulation we cannot go on

simply to analyse its basis without considering the various standard explanations given for it. There are several.

1. There is the one which simply ascribes all this to inherently barbaric and predatory character of Nigerian people rooted in our racial genes. Sometimes this is extended to all Africans and black people.
2. A second explanation is one which has it that this sort of conflict is an inevitable part of the process of development towards a modern nation-state like
3. Those of North America and Western Europe; and gradually with more schools, television sets, magazine, graduates and suburbs we shall grow-out of it as these other 'developed countries' have all done.
4. A third explanation which, like the second, used to be dominant in the political science department, but might not still be, is the ethnic competition for scarce resources by modernising elites.
5. The fourth one is that such developments are part of the growth of cultural awareness and assertion among the   non-westernised section of Nigeria which the westernised sections would resist but ultimately succumb to.

'The Nigerian Character' Hypothesis

The first explanation which may be called 'the Nigerian character hypothesis' can be dismissed as racist nonsense. It merely expresses the refusal of the ruling classes of neo-colonial Africa to admit their total incapacity to maintain even the neo-colonial structures at a tolerable level of efficiency. Instead of admitting their incapacity, they look in our people for congenital, inherited, character defects, just as their mentors, the colonialists, have always done. The 'Nigerians are ungovernable!' cry is part of this attempt to deny politics and economics and go for psychology and genetics, and thus to refuse facing the brute fact of a *system*, which is inherently and congenially corrupt and inefficient.

The Stages-of-Growth Theory

The second explanation, the stages-of-growth explanation, is contradicted by the evidence in North America and Western Europe, whose societies are supposed to typify the most advanced stage yet reached by humanity. North America may be seen as a pot, but no serious melting has taken place in it; at some levels a process of freezing is more discernible. Both American and Canadian societies are seething with religious and ethnic tensions and conflicts of the most multifarious kind, whose significance, the other well-known myth, of pluralism, cannot hide. The ethos, politics and even dialect pattern of New York, Chicago, Boston and Montreal, for example, leave no doubt about this.

But Belgium is perhaps the best example of the fallacy of the stages-of-growth theory. It was one of the first countries to industrialise and establish a bourgeois democratic system. It is right now one of the most highly industrialised countries of the world; a key hub of the European Common Market; high on all the 'growth' indices, from colour television to suicide; from antibiotics per capita to old people per capita. But right now Belgium is racked with tension and conflict over the use of the languages of the Flemish and Walloon ethnic groups. This conflict is also a Catholic *versus* Protestant one. There is no need to mention

Great Britain with its Scottish, Welsh and Irish problems. All these of course are normally explained as further evidence of the inevitability of ethnicity; and the revised version of the inevitability of instability thesis. It is always of course never the instability of the wealth, property and privilege of this bourgeoisie, but of the nation. The former gets more stabilised – abroad!

The Competition for Scarce Resources Rationalisation

The hypothesis that all such religious and ethnic conflicts are part of the inevitable competition for scarce resources by modernising ethnic elites is perhaps the most popular in this country. It was at one time almost the official ideology of this university, especially our Faculty of Arts and Social Sciences. It is still very powerful, widely held and disseminated. This is largely because it seems to provide a scientific and rational justification for what would otherwise appear for what it is – sordid, self-aggrandisement. For according to this hypothesis if one gets a plot at Victoria Island, or a directorship, a Mercedes or some shares, one is getting a share of the scarce resources of the country on behalf of an ethnic or religious group one is supposed to belong to. Private greed and accumulation, legal and illegal, is rationalised in smooth American social science jargon. Gifts, a pittance of what the modernising elite loots, at local functions and to individuals, are said to provide an empirical proof of this hypothesis, which is basically one of riding limousine cars and vacationing abroad on behalf of one's tribesmen or co-religionists, who are starving, but somehow vicariously share in the limousine and the luxury! It not only provides a rational basis for corruption of all sorts and

14

stealing, but makes all this part of the eternal order, since according to bourgeois economics, resources are always scarce, and according to bourgeois political science it is the allocation of these which politics is always and everywhere about.

But let us examine the two key premises of this explanation. The first one is that there is a scarcity of resources. The second one that there is a competition for this between modernising elites.

In our country the basic resources of labour, land, water, fauna and flora are, far from being scarce, abundant in an almost absolute sense. What is scarce is the utilisation of these resources. Or more accurately, the organisation for their utilisation. The first premise is clearly false.

What about the second premise? Is there any competition between modernising elites? A few days ago the annual public accounts of the Metal Box Company were published in the papers. One of the directors is called Mr. Silas Daniyan and another is called Alhaji Shehu Malami. One is Mr. Silas and the other is Alhaji Shehu. Are they involved in any competition in Metal Box boardrooms? This is presumably what we are supposed to believe. We are supposed to believe that Mr. Silas is somehow representing Christians and Alhaji Shehu, somehow, the Muslims, and they compete in Metal Box to obtain scarce resources for the ethno-religious communities their names ascribe to them. Far from competing, every evidence indicates that they co-operate fully, as they have the same interest in playing their role of 'local nationals', as Sir Alex Page, the chairman of the mother Metal Box company in Britain, calls them, then he reported on

15

how highly profitable the Nigerian market has been for the company.

Take those people who got commission from Leyland for the buses and shared it out among themselves. Were they competing in any way with each other? In all the reports of the probes published, hundreds of millions of naira were involved, but what is the single shred of evidence that any competition hampered the deals through which public wealth was looted? The evidence is of co-operation and collusion, and where there was conflict, it had nothing to do, even as a preference, with ethnicity, religion, but hard cash and individual greed. And this happened right across the country. There is now substantial documentation of the operation of this system for at least the period 1970-75, I challenge all those who hold and disseminate the theory of competition for scarce resources on behalf of ethnic and religious groups to show any evidence of it from these or any other body of documents! What is quite clear is that there was competition, but this was between the interest of the common people of this country, on the one hand, and avaricious private interests of intermediaries right across the country and their capitalist principals right across the world, on the other.

The Cultural Awareness and Assertions Myth

The fourth explanation for this pattern of events, that it is an expression of growing cultural awareness by non-westernised groups, is easy to see through. This can be done just by trying to discover the cultural content in these assertions. One of the most striking features of the assertions and posturing by these so-called defenders of a non-western culture, is that they are empty of culture, non-western or,

16

western. But they are full of humbug and hypocrisy and other sentiments which are now adays scraped up to cover the greed and neuroses of the more insecure fractions of Nigeria's dependent bourgeoisie. But culture, as that dimension of human existence dealing with fundamental conceptions and values and their communication and expression (except in its neo-colonial residue form); is completely absent from these assertions and 'awareness'. Even the posturings in defence of non-westernised culture, take the form of a caricature of western orientalists and anthropologists protecting pristine native cultures.

The Real Basis of the Manipulation

If all these standard and conventional explanations for this pattern of events are false and mystifying, what then is its real basis? In order to get to this we have to start our analyses with the meaning of manipulation.

If the meaning of manipulation is *controlling the action of a person or group without that person or group knowing the goals, purpose and method of that control and without them being aware that a form of control is being exercised on them at all,* then an essential precondition for it is ignorance on the part of those who are being manipulated. But ignorance of what? It is impossible to keep a group of people, especially those belonging to the productive classes, ignorant of all aspects of social and political reality. So it has to be ignorance of some aspects of reality. But, then what particular aspect?

The particular aspect of social and political reality to be obscured and mystified depends on the purpose of the manipulation. It also depends on the structure of the economy and society within which this manipulation is taking

17

place. In the case of the manipulation of religion in Nigeria today the purpose of this manipulation is to be found in the purposes and function of the classes who do this manipulation. Nobody denies that the class responsible is the intermediary bourgeoisie. This class is created to serve as the link and intermediary between the people and the wealth of Nigeria and the world capitalist system. It is created to serve as the leading agent of the trading-post which has been and still is Nigeria. It can only continue to be dominant if Nigeria remains a trading-post; that is a trading-post, built to export raw materials and import manufactured goods and services; a trading-post where ownership and consumption and *not* production are dominant in the whole system.

What I want to get across is that an intermediary bourgeois, whether a contractor, financier, bureaucrat, academic, landlord, owner of assembly plants, or transporter lives by appropriating goods and values for consumption which he plays no role in creating. He is a broker, a middleman, socially, economically and culturally! He embodies the domination of appropriation over creation; consumption over production. Far from contributing to the creation of material goods, services, or even functioning social and political values and structures, he survives on shortages and blockages in production just as in communication and understanding. He is the quintessential gateman! This is true of the sleek fat cat as it is of the lean cat trying to get fat.

Can this sort of person come out and frankly ask the people to follow him for what he is? So that he can take a piece of paper from one bank to another; from one factory to another, and make millions? What I mean is that the intermediary bourgeois will cease to exist once the people can see clearly what his true nature is. Can anybody come out and say 'vote for me so that I can get contracts and build foreign bank accounts and houses with my foreign partners? Or follow me and listen to me so that I can get a plot at Ikoyi or Bompai and get a directorship and shares in U.A.C. or Leventis'? Or, 'follow me so that I can get a big job and you can derive the satisfaction that, although you do not have one square meal a day and your daughter is deformed by and dying of chronic malaria, I am eating dinner costing ₦15.00 at Federal Palace Suites Hotel on your behalf and that of others in our tribe and religion'? Can anybody come out and say that? No! That is why this class has to obscure its true role and function in our political economy. You cannot stand and win elections, even if the Electoral College is only two dozen councillors, on the platform that you want to own houses in Ikoyi or London.

What I am getting at is that the intermediary bourgeois cannot appear as what he really is in the political economy of Nigeria. He has to find a cover. He cannot claim political leadership openly on the grounds that he is, or wants to be, an exporter-importer, a contractor, commission-agent, shareholder, rentier or rich bureaucrat. He has to take cover as a Muslim or Christian. He has to take cover as an Ibo, Hausa, Idoma or Efik. He has to take on disguises. He has to posture as a 'majority' or a 'minority'. The manipulation of religion in Nigeria today is essentially a means of creating the context for this fancy-dress ball, for this charade of disguises. This game of masks!

Conclusion

The real basis of the manipulation of religion, in Nigeria today is the need to obscure from the people of Nigeria a fundamental aspect of our reality: that is the domination of our political economy by a class of intermediaries who are being increasingly exposed. And this is to enable this class to cover themselves with religious and ethnic disguises In order to further entrench division among our people, slow down their awakening, at any cost; even the unity of our country, for which so much has been sacrificed.

Recently, some of you students, here in the campuses in Zaria and Kano, became active agents of this pattern of manipulation. This is mainly through the way you have defined the issues in your elections. It might appear to you that joining in this manipulation is doing something new, avant-garde and profoundly political. It might well seem to you that you are taking part in some really advanced strategic or tactical operation, etc. You might not be old enough to know, but a lot of you should, that what you are doing is retrograde in a really tragic sense. It has all been done before, here in this country, and its bankruptcy became so blatant. There was a political organisation known as the Non-Muslim League. The N.P.C. and U.M.B.C., A.G. and most of the other parties made the same assertions and posturing that some of you are making on religion; that is over twenty years ago and they did not get anywhere, except into confusion.

Far from engaging in anything unique,; you are doing what every cheap imperialist huckster has done and is still doing – using religion to confuse and destabilise. Right now it is being done in Egypt, Ethiopia, Tanzania, Sudan, and other countries around the world. For some of you there is, I think, no likelihood that you will ever appreciate that you are playing this role. But most of you may face up to the reality, the hard brutal facts of our social and economic reality. You may face up to these honestly, and up to the consequences, as to where your duty and responsibility lies. You may refuse and follow the parade and march-past of all parasitical and retrograde forces into the dung-heap of history. The choice is not going to be indefinitely open to you. But whatever you choose our people are going inevitably towards their total liberation. The manipulation of religion in Nigeria today can only waste time, a little time.

Notes

1. These three were governors of North-West State, Plateau State, and North-Central State holding the ranks of Assistant Commissioner of Police, Commissioner of Police and Army Brigadier respectively when the Gowon regime was toppled. Along with the other nine military and police governors they were dismissed with ignominy and ten million naira worth of their domestic assets confiscated. This was announced by Murtala in a nation-wide broadcast on 3rd February 1976. What finally provoked the forces of reaction to mount their rebellion against Murtala's government was this part of the broadcast. Murtala said:'...all the ex-military governors and the former administrator of East-Central State, with the exception of two, were found to have grossly abused their office and guilty of several irregular practices. Clearly (the) investigation has revealed that they had betrayed the trust and confidence reposed in them by the nation. Those of them who wore uniform betrayed the ethics of their profession and they are a disgrace to these professions. They should be ashamed of themselves. They are therefore all dismissed with

21

ignominy and with immediate effect. Where the public officers have not been able to explain satisfactorily their earnings and assets, these have been confiscated. In addition, the Ministry of Justice and Police will look into the necessary legal action If need be.' What made this even more threatening was that a White Paper, setting out the decisions of the government on the findings of the panel which investigated these governors, federal commissioners and officials was issued immediately *(New Nigerian* 9th February 1976 and 10th February 1976). Among the intentions mentioned in the White Paper were the decisions:

a) To investigate the overseas assets of all the governors and federal commissioners;

b) To investigate the domestic and overseas assets of their associates and of 'certain individuals who grew rich overnight'.

c) To carry out further investigations into the assets of some senior serving or retired officers of the government not included in those already investigated.

Within ten days of this broadcast, Murtala was assassinated. See the lecture on Murtala Muhammed Memorial Day (in *For The Liberation of Nigeria)* for a discussion of the significance of these decisions announced on 3rd February 1976.

2. One of the most voluminous examples of this type of outlook is the thesis of Mahmud Mohammed Tukur, former Vice-Chancellor of Bayero University, Kano: *Values and Public Affairs: the Relevance of the Sokoto Caliphate Experience to the Transformation of the Nigerian Polity* (Ahmadu Bello University, Zaria, 1977). His views and those of Chike Obi, Professor of Mathematics at the University of Lagos, essentially constitute complementary variants on the same theme. See *New Nigerian,* 5th August, 1978.

II. NATIONAL COHESION, NATIONAL PLANNING AND THE CONSTITUTION*

This conference is on issues in the Draft Constitution. One important issue which does not feature in the list of topics on the agenda of this conference and generally in the debate on the constitution is that of national cohesion. There is a general failure to deal directly with the issue of how to provide in a constitution the formal basis and framework for national cohesion and for national planning to further forge this cohesion. For national cohesion has to be planned for deliberately and consciously, as it cannot come about through accident or luck no matter how many centuries a people band together within one sovereignty[1].

The issue of national cohesion is important because without forging much greater cohesion at all levels we cannot use even one-tenth of one per cent of all our resources to improve the miserable living conditions of our people. Without much greater national cohesion we cannot build the social, economic, and political foundations on which to promote and defend our dignity and independence and indeed our survival as one country. Some people are beginning to take the survival of this country for granted, ignoring or refusing to face up to the existence of powerful forces of disunity, disintegration and confusion which will stop at nothing to delay and block the total liberation of this

---

*Paper presented at the National Conference on Issues in the Draft Constitution at the Institute of Administration, Ahmadu Bello University, Zaria, 21st-24th March, 1977. This paper was published in *Issues in the Draft Constitution*, edited by S. Kumo and A. Aliyu, Zaria, 1977, In the *New Nigerian*, 29th March, 1977, and in *For The Liberation of Nigeria*, New Beacon Books, London, 1979.

continent: And the most effective weapon of those forces is the manipulation of ethnic and religious differences, especially in countries like ours.

It seems clear that the level of national cohesion in this country is very low and has to be much higher. I wish there was enough time to examine in detail the present state of this at the economic, social and political levels[2]. But even if we cannot do that, the significance of this comes out everywhere we look.

On the C.D.C., for example, one of the most prominent, but implicit, arguments against any constitutional proposals, which provide for fundamental changes in the economic and social structure of this country, is that our unity is too fragile. And, therefore, anything which upsets the status quo is dangerous; but that by accepting the status quo we can gradually modify things and become more united and ultimately become like America. The fact that it was the fairly drastic changes, carried out after 29th July, 1975, which actually provided sufficient national cohesion for the whole attempt at building a democratic system, is completely ignored. Also ignored is the fact that commitment to the preservation of the status quo by the Gowon regime is what seriously undermined the little amount of national cohesion attained after the successful resolution of the secession crisis. Indeed our historical experience under Balewa, Ironsi and Gowon shows that succumbing to the status quo by any government subverts our cohesion and is almost criminal.

A constitution produced by the majority of the members of the C.D.C. has provided in Article 2 that:

'Nigeria is one indivisible and indissoluble sovereign State...'[3]

And in Article 9 that:

> 'The motto, of the Republic shall be UNITY AND FAITH, PEACE AND PROGRESS and accordingly national integration shall be actively encouraged whilst discrimination on the grounds of place of origin, religion, sex, status, ethnic or linguistic association or ties shall be prohibited.'

Under these articles it is *made* the duty of the State to encourage free mobility of people, goods and services; ensure residence rights for all citizens everywhere; promote inter-ethnic, inter-religious and inter-linguistic associations and even inter-marriage!! There are other innumerable exhortations about promoting national unity, commanding national loyalty; 'national loyalty to override sectional loyalties', feeling of belonging, etc.

It is presumably in order to ensure all this laboriously expressed commitment that they provide in Article 123 that:

> 'Appointments to the office of Minister of the Government of the Federation shall be made by the President acting in his discretion...and...at least one Minister of the Government of the Federation shall be appointed from among Nigerian citizens who belong to each of the States comprising the Federation.'

And it is also for the same purpose that they provide in Article 173 that:

> 'the members of the executive committee or other governing body of a political party shall be deemed to reflect, the federal character of Nigeria only if the members belong to different states not being less in

number than two-thirds of all the states comprising the Federation.'

The crucial words in these provisions are clearly *belongs to*. These are defined in Article 210 which states that 'belongs to when used with reference to a state refers to a person either of whose parents was a member of a community indigenous to that state.'

The most important issue, with regard to all these two provisions in Articles 123 and 173, is therefore: *what exactly constitutes 'a community indigenous to a State?* It is on this issue that the whole import of the provisions hangs. Has a community got to come from nowhere else for it to be indigenous to a place? Or if emigration is allowed, for how many generations has a family got to stay in a place to become indigenous? Who are the indigenes of Gongola State, for example? Is it the Bachama, who somebody will say came from Gobir? Or the Jukun, who somebody will say came from Egypt? Or the Chamba, who somebody will say came from the Chad? Or the Fulani, who somebody will say came from the Senegal? If it is a matter of length of occupation: how many years have a people got to stay in a place before they become indigenes of the place? One thousand years, five hundred years, one century, just a generation or just one dry season?

Under the draft constitution most of the ministers appointed by the president would have to publish their genealogies with a commentary and probably face court action to prove their indigeneity. How many of the federal commissioners would face court action if they had to prove that they are indigenous to a state?

It would not only be when ministers are appointed that there would be litigation and rumpus but indeed every time a political party registers the names of its executive committee. There would be national debates and discussion on their origin, the origin of their grandmothers, grandfathers, and even on the indigeneity of the communities they claim to come from. There shall be very lucrative business for us in history fabricating and exposing genealogies, and for lawyers carrying out the litigation and evolving a body of law unique to Nigeria and built on the solid foundation of our cherished traditions and culture!

Not only does it make ethnicity – indeed a deepened form of ethnicity akin to racism – a permanently explosive political issue, but it completely makes bogus the provision of full residence rights, free mobility, and completely undermines the development of national citizenship, a basic requirement for national cohesion. By reducing participation in the political system to crudely racist levels, it establishes three distinct types of Nigerian citizens.

The first-class citizens are those who live in a state where they can claim to belong to 'a community indigenous to that state'. The second-class citizens are those who can claim origin from 'a community indigenous' in one of the states but actually live in another. These citizens may carpetbag to their 'state of origin' if they want to fully participate in the political system these people are proposing. The third class citizens are those who cannot claim to belong to 'a community indigenous' to any of the states, although they are full-fledged Nigerian citizens. The confusion and dissention this is going to cause is not just going to extend to the people of Ibo, Hausa, Efik or Nupe origin living in Lagos,

27

Ibadan or Port Harcourt or just to the people of Yoruba origin in Kaduna, Jos, Kano or Makurdi. It is going to extend to the Kanuri, Sakkwatawa and Nupe in Jimeta. It is going to extend to the Jassawa of Kano origin; the inhabitants of Ibadan of Igbirra, Igala, Hausa, Ijebu or Benin origin; to the Fulani of Bida and llorin; the people of Marghi origin in Gongola, and to millions of Nigerian citizens, the movements of whose parents and grandparents over centuries has woven the real fabric on which national citizenship and cohesion may be forged. The confusion and dissention would certainly give us a political system like that of America which is what these people want – but it would not move us towards national cohesion for another millennium.

If our draft constitution had been published you would have seen an alternative to this confusion. We propose in Article 104 that federal ministers should simply be members of the National Assembly and therefore members of a national political party, with no other restriction. Over the composition of the executive councils of a national political party we propose as Article 41 (e) that such a party must have, to obtain recognition:

'Among members of its national executive organ and its principal officers at least one eligible voter domiciled in each of the sixteen states of the Federal Republic of Nigeria.'

We do not propose the creation of special classes of Nigerian citizens or reduce our political system to the level of genetics and biology as these people do. But that is probably why some of the members of the C.D.C. are so vehement against the publication of our critique and alternative proposals, as it would show clearly the disastrous course they are proposing for this country.

Religion

As I have already pointed out their constitution is full of grand pronouncements about national unity, national integration and national loyalty overriding sectional loyalties. But far from proposing a basis and framework for these they have provided the framework for the manipulation of ethnic and religious differences. This also comes out clearly on the question of religion, the state and the law.

If there is one thing which is so openly essential for ensuring the forging of national cohesion it is separating the Nigerian state clearly and unambiguously from religion and ensuring that its function is to protect the right of citizens to practice the religious belief of their choice. But the only provision which touches it in their draft, is the limp and watery one in Article 17 which states 'The State shall not adopt any religion as the State religion'. This clearly allows the state to be associated, identified or linked with any religion as long as this stops short of adoption. This provision can only have been proposed with the deliberate intention of allowing the president, the governors and other public officers to manipulate religious differences by associating or identifying with religion. Otherwise, knowing fully well the chaos that has been caused in this country because political parties and governments have cynically manipulated religious belief, they have no excuse whatsoever for not being unambiguous and categorical on this matter. Again if our draft constitution had been published you would have seen an alternative to such an ambiguous and dubious treatment of a key and volatile issue. In Article 39 of our draft, we have stated that:

> 'The Federal Republic of Nigeria is a secular state and the state, shall not be associated with any religion but shall actively protect the fundamental right of all citizens to hold and practice the religious beliefs of their choice.'

The reason why I believe that the failure of the C.D.C. majority to come out unambiguously on this issue is a deliberate one is because of the provisions of Article 11 of their draft. This provides that every citizen shall have equality of rights, obligations and opportunities before the law as long as it does not:

> 'Invalidate a rule of Islamic law or customary law'.

This exemption is apparently intended to ensure that the provisions of the Sharia and customary law over inheritance and other such matters of personal law are not made invalid. But in fact this exemption is a complete sham because these matters come before courts of law and this Article is *non-justiciable* and therefore cannot be applied in any court of law. Furthermore the exemption is unnecessary since it is provided in the section over fundamental rights of belief. But its inclusion serves the purpose of making religion a divisive political issue and this has been done quite cynically even to the extent of not including the laws and codes of the numerous Christian denominations which are certainly not the same thing as the British Common Law applied in the high courts and others. With one stroke the ethos of justice and equality for all citizens, the only basis for building national cohesion, has been undermined and a basis for religious dissension, not only between major religions but among religious sects has been introduced. This perfectly well serves the purpose of all those who want to manipulate religious differences to entrench or to win political power. It also serves, perfectly, the foreign interests in places like Saudi Arabia, Kuwait, the United States and Europe who systematically and in a coordinated fashion use Islamic and Christian missionary and 'African' religious organisations to block and delay the forging of national cohesion in any part of the African continent where religious differences are susceptible to manipulations. These foreign interests appear on the surface to be divided and in rivalry but whether they are in the United States or in its client states like Saudi Arabia and Kuwait they work for exactly the same ends. They are working to prevent the total liberation of Africa and the collapse of the western capitalist system, at least in Europe and the Middle East, which will inevitably follow.

National Political Parties

A constitution which is intended to provide a framework for national unity and cohesion must take seriously into account the existence of these forces and other foreign forces who actively seek to manipulate and control our institutions for divisive ends. The most important of the new institutions, to be created by a new constitution they will seek to control, are the political parties. And this will be done, as has been done before with the N.P.C., N.C.N.C., Action Group, N.E.P.U. and the old parties, mainly through control of party funds and resources. This particular draft constitution does not provide any serious measures to prevent this. The provision in Article 175 is again completely useless because it only provides for the forfeiture of funds

31

send directly from another country. They do not attempt to control and limit *all contributions* to party funds. This is the only way to prevent such secret funding. It is well known that most of the old political parties did not get their funds directly from abroad. They got them through companies and other institutions operating in this country and through Nigerians who have legitimate connections with these. The only way to prevent such dangerous foreign manipulation of our politics is by limiting *all contributions* to political parties to specific amounts and only from eligible voters. It would then not be possible for a company, a religious organisation, a youth, 'students' or trade union body to be used as a conduit for foreign funds. Even if it is, it would be much easier to discover with the other provisions of open accounting and regular auditing. But they do not provide for this at all. But we propose in Article 41 (b) of our draft that for a political party to gain and retain recognition, it must have:

'its funds derived entirely from the contributions of eligible voters which is limited for any one calendar year and for any eligible voter to the amount of a candidate's deposit to the Federal House of Repre-sentatives.'

Executive President

The justification they give for making the office of president so powerful is that he will provide effective govern-ment and become a focus of national loyalty. But it is not clear how this effectiveness and loyalty will develop if there are no provisions to ensure that the president will be elected and operate during his term as somebody who, with his team, stands for a definite political programme and policies. Unless

32

this is ensured the president will be seen as standing for nothing more than his personality and ultimately his place of origin. One of the major shortcomings of the Gowon regime which made it so incapable of maintaining or mobilising any support is the way the leadership was personalised both at the Federal and State levels. Towards the end, the head of state and the governors stood for nothing but themselves and the cliques of crooks around them. When, after 29th July, 1975, the new leadership came out and adhered to a programme and played down considerably the personality of the leaders this made them far more effective and respected. The image of collective leadership and decision-making and the reduced emphasis on personality and more on policy and programme made a lot of difference, not only to the formulation of policy but to the ability to recognise mistakes and change drastically as they did in November 1975 over Angola.

A constitution therefore should ensure the emergence of a leadership on which personality is clearly subsidiary to policy and programme. This can only be done by ensuring that the president and governors can only be elected on the platform of a national political party and are clearly identified with a specific political programme. The majority of the C.D.C. make no such provisions. According to their proposals the president or anybody for that matter does not have to go to a political party before standing for elections. In spite of the elaborate provisions for national political parties, these parties are not made essential in the political process. What they provide for are actually election campaign organisations developing around a politician which will masquerade as national political parties, but will in fact be no such thing and amount to a collection of hacks and sycophants.

In our own draft constitution we provide for that and indeed for the democratic nomination of candidates and the democratic formulation of the party programme. We also provide for collective decision-making at all levels not just at the party level. Without provisions to ensure this, the president and the governors will, far from being a focus of loyalty and effective leaders, be merely power-hungry, megalomaniac political operators whose personality and ego will be the most prominent aspects of their governments. Such political leaders will only create national disunity because, ultimately, the personality, no matter what national garb it is sold in at the elections, will come out with its ethnic and religious colouring. The provision regarding the appointment of ministers, purely at the discretion of the president, who will represent ethnic communities indigenous to each of the nineteen states ensures this process; and reduces the significance of policy and programme and places all emphasis on personality and, basically, origin.

National Planning

Not only are their proposals regarding fundamental principles and objectives and major political institutions and offices geared against national cohesion, but they fail to provide the basis and organs for national planning, which are essential for the conscious promotion of national cohesion.

The establishment of a uniform land tenure system is one crucial basis for proper and comprehensive national planning. It is a necessary basis even if one only wants to plan to ensure the even and balanced distribution of the parasitical capitalist class throughout the country. But the majority of the C.D.C. have opposed any such move. This is because in present circumstances this uniformity can only come about by the abolition of private land-ownership in the southern states and reallocation of plots on an equitable principle all over the country. Their report reveals the violent temper which the mere proposal of reallocation of plots on an equitable basis provoked. In Section 3.6-1 of their report they state:

'It is therefore obnoxious, immoral, unethical and wholly unjustifiable to take away through the Constitution by way of mandatory provisions vested rights of a citizen which he lawfully acquired and for which there is no state necessity or need. This is confiscatory in concept though dressed in a different garb.'

To protect against any 'confiscation' of their property and the property of those they represent, the majority of the C.D.C. went ahead and in the *justiciable* part of the constitution enshrined and entrenched the right to private property. Article 36, in which this is done, is one of the longest and most tightly worded articles of the constitution. It is so tight that it is impossible for the government to plan anything which involves the use of land. Not even their Article 26 which provides for the right to life, which is all that the great majority of Nigerians have, is so long or tightly worded. Not only did they entrench this right to private accumulation of property but went ahead and in the next article provided that:

'No person other than a Nigerian citizen shall own absolute interest in land.'

Why anybody, whether a Nigerian or not, should hold absolute right in land, when nobody's father, grandfather or great-grandfather has created land beats one's imagination. It is very revealing here that those people who mention the name of God in every other sentence have not come in here to explain to them that God created land and nobody has any business claiming absolute right in it. It is blasphemous.

But of course the Nigerian bourgeois always believes that he is God-sent as he makes his fortune or career so miraculously, with such ease!

If our draft had been published you would have seen an alternative proposal regarding land ownership, which is not state and bureaucratic control and confiscations. We propose in Article 34 that:

'The Federal Republic of Nigeria shall within the framework of this constitution treat with special urgency and determination the question of land ownership and control and resolve it in the interests of the peasant farmers and tenants on the principle that land shall be owned and controlled by those who work and live on it.'

We also provide for the protection and encouragement of *legitimate* and socially beneficial accumulation of private property. In Article 37 of our draft we propose that:

'Every citizen is entitled as a fundamental right to own and use the products of his physical and mental labour except the portion which is utilised by public institutions for the general welfare of the community and the nation.'

Our own proposals regarding the organisation of production and the distribution of income from production are set within a clear definite framework quite different from the clichés about public ownership of the means of production, distribution and exchange. This simply means nationalisation and in most parts of the world this is simply a rationalisation of exploitation and private accumulation by and through bureaucrats and managers. In Article 6 we provide the general principle that:

> '... all the resources of this country belong to the people of this country and shall under the direction of the state be entirely utilised for even, balanced and self-reliant national development in order to promote the welfare of all the people and build a just and egalitarian society free from the exploitation of man by man.'

This is set out more specifically in Article 33 which provides that:

> 'The Federal Republic of Nigeria is committed to fostering the establishment of just social relations in all sectors of production and in all spheres of society and therefore shall especially support and protect the interests of the peasant farmers, nomads, artisans, petty traders, and wage earners and shall also develop genuine produce and consumer co-operatives and collectives.'

Within this framework national political parties may disagree as to the best method of achieving them. But they provide the only viable basis of national cohesion because they are promoting and defending the interest of the overwhelming majority of the people. The C.D.C. on the other hand propose a basis of consensus which promotes and defends the interest of a tiny bourgeois elite and their imperialist masters, and on this very narrow basis national cohesion cannot be built. Not only because this leaves almost all Nigerian citizens to the dogs, but because this elite and its masters are predatory in their greed and will always remain torn by rivalries and conflict and are completely incapable of building a cohesive nation, not just within our lifetime, but even that of our great-grandchildren.

Indeed there can be no planning with the type of economy they are proposing. In their great wisdom they choose *Cooperative Federalism*. The profound and mature thought and consideration which went into the choice of *Cooperative Federalism* is admirable. For it involves making the very difficult choice between *Cooperate* and *Non-Cooperative* Federalism! But it is difficult to see why they did not go ahead and provide the Federal Government with the powers and organs to even plan for this Cooperative Federalism. In Article 10 they provide that:

'The State shall direct its policy towards ensuring the promotion of planned and balanced economic development.'

This is followed by other such grand pronouncements about what shall be provided for the welfare of the citizen. But all this is simply bogus. Because the only national planning organs provided (Article 136) are the National Economic Council and the National Economic Planning Committee. And these have only powers to *coordinate* the nineteen separate state plans. Our proposals on this are quite different. For while fully taking into account the need for autonomy and initiative for the state and local government councils we provide the basis and organs for comprehensive and proper national planning.

Conclusion

It seems quite clear that, if their constitution is adopted, far from moving towards national cohesion Nigeria will become torn with ethnic and religious disunity and sectionalism. Far from providing a basis and framework for the development of national cohesion and democracy, there will be an intensification of the present grossly uneven pattern of underdevelopment, greater capitalist and bureaucratic greed, individualism and chaos. When that happens the Nigerian people will be accused of being too immature and irresponsible for democracy and preparation will be made for consolidating the status quo and ensuring 'law and order' through repression and terror. From the individualism, greed, chaos and thuggery of capitalist bureaucrats and politicians we shall move to the indiscipline, chaos, individualism, greed and repression of capitalist bureaucrats and soldiers. And all this would be done in the name of national unity and national cohesion which, however, every attempt has been made to block and prevent.

Notes

1. There is this dubious optimism around this country that if we just band together we shall get used to each other and become more united and cohesive. It is argued that with 'development' and 'enlightenment' our people will become more mature and united and the country more stable like Britain, America and the Scandinavian countries. For incisive studies showing the historically-determined nature of British nationality – that is, the absence of any inevitability about the transformation of political communities in Britain, see the writings of Tom Nairn like

his 'Scotland: Anomaly in Europe', *New Left Review*, 83, January-February 1973, pp. 57-82.

2. My views on the present state of this are, briefly, that the defeat of the secessionist movement and the administrative changes this involved have enhanced considerably the authority of the Federal Government. This has increased the administrative cohesion of the country especially since July 1975, when the state governments have been brought more firmly and rationally under the Federal Government. But this cohesion has remained primarily at .the administrative and fiscal levels. The political values, structures and activity which alone can give this substance and momentum do not yet exist. The most powerful groups and forces operating in the public and private institutions are those working for the preservation of the present conditions of low-level integration (or perverse integration), sectional conflict and bargaining. One of the major features of the Nigerian situation in the next decade is the struggle between these groups and forces and those others which seek to create political structures, tendencies and activity which forge national cohesion from the village to the national level.

3. *Report of the Constitution Drafting Committee Containing the (sic) Draft Constitution. Vol. 1.* Lagos, 1976. All the other quotations and references are to the first printing of this.

4. *A Draft Constitution for the Federal Republic of Nigeria: A Minority Submission,* by O. Osoba and Y.B. Usrnan.

August, 1976. AH the other references and quotations are from this mimeographed version.

5. This section is quoted in full on p. 66 of *For the Liberation of Nigeria*.

6. The Action Group, N.P.C. and N.C.N.C. received Israeli, Kuwaiti, and other such imperialist-inspired funding for fostering religious division indirectly through firms, persons and organisations operating in Nigeria. Israeli agencies and their Kuwaiti counterparts did not send cheques 'payable to' A.G. or N.P.C. or pretend that they come from the Tel Aviv or Kuwaiti branches of these parties. Their provisions for keeping out foreign funds therefore are comical and deliberately leave a loophole for the continuation of past practices.

III. THE SUBSTANCE OF THE PROBLEM OF NATIONAL UNITY IN NIGERIA TODAY*

Members of the National Youth Service Corps. The subject of my lecture is the problem of national unity in Nigeria today. This is a very wide subject. Therefore I shall focus attention on an aspect of it. This aspect is the issue of what is the actual substance of this problem. I am doing this because it is necessary to begin to move beyond the various forms in which it has so far been presented.

It is particularly necessary to attempt this move forward here, because the whole of the NYSC scheme of which these lectures are preliminaries is intended to inculcate 'the spirit of nationalism' into you, according to the letter of invitation sent to me. For a scheme intended to do this, a definition of the substance of the problem of national unity should be of some significance.

Of course, there are many people in the governments, business companies, armed forces, and the universities, in this country who are hostile towards any attempt at definition and analysis. They would say that all this is a waste of time, what we need is 'action' and 'honesty and sincerity', they may add. Definition, analyses and theory, they would say are useless, and at most should be confined to the classrooms and campuses, for they emanate from 'foreign ideology'. They may be saying this on their way back from the United States Congress, or from the banks, boardrooms

---

*Lecture to members of the National Youth Service Corps, Orientation Course, Kaduna, Wednesday, 20th August, 1980.

42

and shops of Rome, Geneva, London, Tokyo, or even Kuwait and Hong Kong, but they would say it with a perfectly straight face and in all seriousness, until you insist on being told the exact objective of this 'action' they are urging, especially for the majority of the people of this country, and what precisely it is we should be 'honest' and 'sincere' about. Then this primitive, dependent, and reactionary mentality, so pervasive in this country, will express itself in threats and abuse, or in silence, or laughter, depending on your relative positions. We cannot allow this country to continue to be dragged along at this very backward level of the understanding of the world and of society.

Appearance and Substance

But we cannot really move forward, towards a better understanding of the problem of national unity in our country, or of any phenomenon, for that matter, without first distinguishing the appearance of the problem and its substance. This distinction between what something appears to be, and what it actually is and what determines the direction in which it changes, is central to any form of rational knowledge, whether about natural or social phenomena; about physical objects or human beings. You cannot understand the life of birds from their feathers; or of trees from their bark; or the nature of a human being from his or her dress. In order to understand them, and how they change, you have to penetrate into the substance of their structure and constitution. Even the substance of a person's activity, you cannot tell from his words, gestures and statements, no matter how expressive these are. The most fiery and violent rhetoric directed against something may actually constitute the most important protection for it. While the most gentle, pious and peace-loving words and gestures may lead to, or cover up, the most vicious and repressive actions. The distinction between appearance and substance is very crucial, especially when you are dealing with words, with their power to arouse, mesmerise, obscure, or lull to sleep. You can only understand the real meaning and substance of words and gestures by locating their apparent meaning in the context of specific structures and interests or both individuals and societies and their movement.

The issue, or issues, relating to the problems of national unity in Nigeria are being obscured by so many clichés and so many myths. I shall set out briefly three of the most important myths.

Historical Tribalism

The first one may be called the historical tribalism myth. According to this myth, the explanation of the low level of national unity in Nigeria lies in the fact that people in this country used to live as separate tribes each with its 'natural', or 'traditional' ruler or rulers. The tribe, or ethnic group, in these times before colonialism, is said to have been the main political unit, with inter-tribal conflict and warfare as the dominant form of relationship among the peoples of Nigeria. These tribes are seen as being so monolithic that most of them are believed to almost constitute a large family with a single individual as their ancestor. The Hausas with Bayajidda; the Tiv with Takurukuru; the Yoruba with Oduduwa, etc. It is said that after living with this type of social and political system with inter-tribal warfare, inter-tribal enslaving and subjugation, for thousands of years, it shall take a very long time before these previously warring tribes can be united. Through the efforts of the natural rulers and other tribal and community elders, champions and spokesmen, these tribes can be made to live in amity, but it is a very delicate process requiring all the tact and experience and wisdom of these community leaders and champions who are indispensable, as a result of the need for this delicate operation.

This explanation of the problem of national unity has no basis whatsoever in the evidence available of Nigerian historical and contemporary reality, beyond the need for it to preserve the colonial and neo-colonial systems of domination which have come to prevail over the people of Nigeria over the last one hundred and fifty years or so.

In the first place, what are said to be tribes with social, economic, political, and even genealogical cohesion are actually at most linguistic units. This is central to the confusion. It is this linguistic element which is made to appear so comprehensive. The legends, mythology, rumours and hypotheses, arising from the contest for royal office among the ruling classes like those about Bayajidda, Kisra or Oduduwa are then made to appear as evidence of a common ancestry. Not only is this assumption of common ancestry among the people speaking various languages not supported by the scientific evidence available, but it was very rare for one linguistic group to even belong to one pre-colonial sovereign state. Social, and political systems, and systems of economic organisation, have never been coterminous with linguistic units. People speaking the Hausa language, for example, have lived not only under different sovereign states, but even different political systems, extending from the feudal kingdoms like Kebbi and Kano, to the patriarchal city-states like Zoma, Washa and Auyo, down to the sovereign village communities of the valley of the Gulbin Tarka, and the Gwandara, for example. These sovereign village communities in which some Hausa-speaking people lived had social, political and economic systems much closer to those of some of the Ibo-speaking, Edo-speaking, Ijaw-speaking, peoples, than to the patriarchal city-states and feudal kingdoms in which other Hausa-speaking people lived. Not only was there never a single Hausa, Igala, Jukun, Efik or Yoruba sovereign state or even confederation, in spite of the myths about '*ebi*' or 'the sons of Bawo', but there is no evidence that the systems of political organisation under which people speaking some languages lived were similar beyond some terminological affinities.

Far from these tribes existing as great families led by benevolent rulers and wise elders, almost all of them were divided into distinct social groups, in many cases, social classes. These distinctions extended from those of the sovereign village communities with their early and later lineages, settlers and natives, captives and freemen; to the highly stratified societies of feudal kingdoms like Oyo, Katsina, Benin, Onitsha, Igala, Borno and Wukari, with serfs, slaves, free peasants, merchants, and nobilities of theocratic, military and bureaucratic types. Far from inter-tribal warfare being the dominant form of relations, it is these internal social and political relations between individuals, groups and classes belonging to the same linguistic groups and the same societies which determined even these cases of warfare between different political units. These systems kept changing, sometimes gradually, sometimes drastically and in a

46

revolutionary fashion. The political alignments involved were determined by the concrete social and economic interests and circumstances, and not the affinities of kinship and language, as the historical tribalism myth would have us believe. If there is a problem of ethnicity in Nigeria today it is certainly not because these ethnic groups existed before the colonial conquest. The contemporary tribes and ethnic groups of Nigeria, as concepts and units of political action today, never existed in any real historical past of the peoples of this country.

The Psychological Myth

The second body of myth pertains to the psychology of groups and individuals. It is said that people belonging to particular linguistic groups are innately lazy, selfish, honest, crooked, aggressive, or stupid as the case may be. This is sometimes extended to individual political leaders identified with a particular linguistic group, as is currently illustrated by the Awolowo bogey being propagated now.

But while it is true that these characteristics can be found in a person, the explanation for them has to be located not at the level of the language he speaks, but at the level of a given social structure, within which alone selfishness, laziness, aggression, dishonesty and stupidity can exist and form part of a character. The Ibadan artisan and Ekiti peasant cannot rationally be ascribed a certain psychological make-up because they use a common means of expression. It is certainly possible for them to be mobilised to serve the economic and political interest of a professor from Ondo through the manipulation of their conception of what their interests are. Similarly, Kano merchants and Kano workers may share some social and political characteristics, but the explanation for this has to be sought in the structure of society and economy of Kano and not in some psychological trait which is genealogically communicated and not socially acquired. An explanation which is based on genealogically-transmitted psychological traits, as the expressions 'an Ibo-man is always an Iboman'; 'a Hausaman is always lazy'; 'you cannot trust a Yorubaman'; 'a Tivman will always steal', would have it, have no scientific foundation whatsoever but have strong racialist credentials, and those who propagate them should logically extend their implication outside Nigeria and make it global, 'a blackman is always a black-man', and its implications.

The Development and Management Myth

The third myth is that the problems of national unity in Nigeria exists because our economy is backward and our level of management is poor. It is argued that with rising prosperity and economic development, all this shall be a thing of the past as is supposed to have happened in the advanced industrialised countries. This argument is false because the countries in whose footsteps we are supposed to be following like America are torn with the most deep-rooted ethnic and sectional tensions and conflicts. These, far from declining, have in these years intensified. The Irish problem in Britain and similar issues in France and Belgium, for example, demonstrate that these footsteps we are following do not at all lead to a solution of the problem of national unity or even to a greater understanding of its dimension. The American record is disastrous, although we only know of its manifestations in the rebellion of the blacks. The tensions, conflicts and segregation between Jews, Italians, Irish, Poles, Wasps and Mexicans, for example, are largely covered up in the media and in the books. The depth and scope of the Irish problem in Britain, not just in Ulster, is also largely covered up and presented merely as IRA violence while in fact every British city and small town has its 'Irish problem' in its ghettoes, docks, factories and pubs.

Towards A Definition

These myths I have sketched out above far from offering an explanation take us away from an understanding of the problem, because they are either based on false evidence or on false concepts.

In the first place, we should be quite clear about the fact that the problem of national unity does not arise because of the fact of the existence in one country of people with different languages and cultures. This plurality has prevailed throughout history. Cultural and linguistic heterogeneity has been far more common to political units than homogeneity. Such heterogeneity has been a factor favouring political, social, economic and cultural progress. The existence of peoples with distinct languages in Nigeria, or any country, is not therefore a problem at all. The problem is in the role these distinctions come to play in the political system. The political role of this heterogeneity is determined by the operations of the economic and social structures of a particular country.

We have a society in Nigeria now which, throughout the country, is divided into distinct social classes, and strata. These classes are composed of people with a common role in the system of production and the exchange of goods and services in the country. These are the fundamental distinc-

49

testing in a most undignified manner, without any complexes, as Fanon would say.

One of these is Chief Abiola, an agent of the notorious American I.T.T. Company, one of the chief financiers of the ruling National Party of Nigeria, and owner of the *Concord* newspapers. He is reported to have a good chance of becoming the party's next Chairman, and perhaps even presidential candidate in 1983. The other Chief Benson, is trying to get himself a commission from a subcontract sought for by a Belgian company, from the I.T.T. in Nigeria. Chief T.O.S. Benson was a Federal Minister under the Balewa regime. They are particularly revealing because they are also, at present, influential leaders of the National Party of Nigeria, and of the Nigerian People's Party, whose accord is supposed to be one of the bases of Shagari's regime and is supposed to have been made in the interest of national unity and stability.

The substance of the problem of national unity is located in the domination of the Nigerian state by these types of parasites whose sole purpose of existence is not to produce or create, but to serve as gatemen, agents and procurers for the multinationals. The contest for this role is all that their politics is about. Tribalism and ethnicity are the masks and disguises.

There are many such concrete examples, especially in the reports of the various commissions of inquiry instituted by Murtala's regime. They are probably not as vivid as the Benson-Abiola example, but they are very illuminating. It is to these that we now have to turn, and to any such concrete materials, not to myths, if we are to understand, and get others to also understand, the substance of the problem of national unity in Nigeria today. Thank you.

The Manipulation of Religion in Nigeria 1977 - 1987

IV. THE CAMPAIGN FOR A WAR WITH LIBYA: AN OPEN LETTER TO THE NATIONAL ASSEMBLY*

Kaduna,
26th January, 1981

Honourable Senators and Representatives:

It has become necessary to write this letter to you, because the current trend in our country's Central African policy has brought us into direct political and military subservience to French imperialism. This situation of actual subservience to French strategic interests in Central Africa is bad enough by itself, but it also seems to be leading our country, sooner or later, into an intra-African war. In this war, our country is going to be primarily pitted against Libya. In this violent conflict Nigeria shall be fighting, basically, to preserve the system of military, political and economic domination .which the French have built in Central Africa, since their invasion of that region, and the imposition of French military bases at Fort Lamy, and Fort Foreau in 1900 A.D.

The hidden facts about this development, and the hidden possibilities of its outcome, point to a carefully worked out NATO plan to deeply divide the OAU, and also to set, again, two leading members of OPEC violently against one another. This will serve two immediate NATO purposes.

---

*Full text of an Open Letter to the Members of the National Assembly, Monday 26th January, 1981. Published in the *New Nigerian*, 29th January, 1981.

strengthened, modern sophisticated equipments purchased, if need be at the expense of our development plans...'

Within four days of this, the *Nigerian Standard* of Wednesday, 14th January 1981, controlled by the Nigerian People's Party, carried the story titled 'F.G. Urged to Liberate Chad from Libyan Grips', reporting that:

'The Federal Government has been called upon to move into the Chadian territory if the Libyan Government fails to move out of the place within a limited time, the former Minister for Steel Development, Mr. Paul Unongo, urged in Lagos yesterday. Mr. Unongo... charged furiously that if there was to be war in this direction, Nigeria should not shy away from waging war against her enemies.'

Besides many other statements along these lines, the Editor of the *New Nigerian*, controlled by the National Party of Nigeria, came out on Saturday, 17th January 1981 with this, placing the issue in clear terms of massive spending on armaments. He said:

'Colonel Gaddafi's irredentist policy that has resulted in Chad (our North-Western neighbour) and Libya entering into some kind of entente cordiale aimed at merging the two countries together must dictate to us the importance of preparedness and making material commitment to matters of defence and national security ... a financially weak Federal Government will have serious problems defending its borders and maintaining internal security.'

The *Sunday Times* of 18th January 1981, controlled by the N.P.N. like its daily sister paper, carried lurid reports of Gaddafi turning all Libyan schools into army training camps. To cap it all, Dr. K.O. Mbadiwe, a Presidential Adviser on National Assembly Affairs, and a former Federal Minister of African Affairs in the old days of the Nkrumah bogey, had this to say in the *Daily Times* of Monday, January 19th, 1981:

'It was his view that the country's borders could only be more protected when the Federal Government received good money to buy modern weapons for the agents. He cited the threat posed by Libyan presence in Chad as an eloquent example of the need to give the centre enough money.'

Your Responsibilities

The power to declare a state of war between Nigeria and any other country is vested by Section 5(3a) of the Constitution in a joint session of your two Houses. But given the rate of the domestic and external manipulation of Nigeria's Central African policy by the NATO powers, particularly French imperialism; given the wealth, power and connections of the African agents of these imperialist powers, inside and outside Nigeria, you, Honourable Senators and Representatives, may wake up one morning and find Nigeria in an actual state of war in Central Africa and the only power you would be left with is to rubber-stamp and approve the war. You would also be left with no alternative but to vote massive funds for armaments and other war preparations, to enable the Nigerian armed forces to defend French imperialist interests in Central Africa and NATO's current global strategy. The arms salesmen commission agents are already on the move.

Initially the disastrous consequences for Nigeria and Africa shall be covered up by all sorts of chauvinistic and racialist propaganda, directed against Arabs in general and Libyans in particular. But all this will not take long before it is exposed, and you Honourable Senators and Representatives shall be held individually, and collectively, responsible by the people of this country, and the whole of Africa, for whatever happens.

You should therefore start investigating, immediately, the whole background, the forces, patterns and context of the developments which have brought Nigeria's Central African policy to the brink of a war with another African country. This investigation should enable you to decide the best course of action, individually and collectively, and also in the process, make the people of Nigeria better informed and better equipped to decide their destiny.

In the course of these investigations I would urge that you start with establishing the facts of the situation in Central Africa and its broader African and world context; and then examine the. feasibility or otherwise of the possibilities indicated above and any others. I would particularly urge that the factual validity of the following five propositions are examined in the course of these investigations.

French Domination

The first proposition is that the greatest and most fundamental danger facing the people of the Central African region is not from Libya, but is French military, political and economic domination. This domination is direct, pervasive

58

and vicious. It is built on a system of French military bases and a French military surveillance and rapid intervention net-work, stretching from Ivory Coast, through Mali, Senegal, Mauritania, Niger, Chad, Cameroons, Gabon, Central African Republic, Zaire to Rwanda and Burundi. The key French military bases with French troops and aircraft occupying them are right now located at Abidjan, Dakar, Bour, Libreville, Owen do and until recently Ndjamena,' formerly Fort Lamy. These French military bases *are* linked with other French military facilities, and specialist military personnel located in all of these countries and in southern France. This network enables the French government under DeGaulle, Pompidou, Giscard or Mitter and to intervene swiftly, and directly, with or without the approval of the African governments, whenever it feels that French imperialist interests are threatened. Most of the present governments of Central Africa were installed and are maintained by this French military presence. The government of President Ahidjo of the Cameroons was installed and is maintained by this presence. The government of President Bongo of Gabon was installed by French paratroopers who, up to this day, occupy the country. The government of President Mobutu of Zaire has been maintained by a series of military interven-tions by NATO, spearheaded by Belgium, and now France, since it was installed in 1965. The most recent of these inter-ventions was in 1978 when France mobilised the troops of its puppet regimes like Senegal, Gabon and Morocco, and provided support, together with America, to maintain the vicious Mobuto dictatorship. Only last year French troops removed Jean Bedel Bokassa in the Central African Republic and replaced him with David Dacko, and continue to occupy that country up to this day. Any serious and responsible consideration of the Central African situation, by patriotic Africans, has to start from this reality and not from a cover-up of these hard and dangerous facts. I submit this proposition for your consideration.

French Interests

The second proposition is that the strategic interests of French imperialism in Africa today is to continue to keep these countries it occupies, or has placed under effective military surveillance, as a special reserve in which it has preferential economic and military privileges. A special French interest in this region is uranium, whose major African mines, outside South Africa and Namibia, are located at Moana in Gabon, Bakouma in Central African Republic and Arlif and Imouraren in Niger. They are all under tight French control and monopoly, with all the dangerous implications to Africa of French-South African nuclear cooperation. France is even attempting to pre-empt any developments which may threaten its interests by encouraging the integration of the Nigerian armed forces into some sort of ECOWAS defence arrangements with the armies of its puppet governments, which are actually mere units of the French armed forces overseas, and have no independent military capability or real political existence. The current Central African policy of the present Nigerian government is very likely to accelerate this integration of West African armed forces in an anti-Libyan crusade under effective, even if not apparent, French umbrella and tutelage. Such an involvement would be dangerous, not just to the sovereignty of Nigeria, but even to its continued existence as a single unit. As a former adviser of President Houphouet Boigny, Jacques Baulin, is reported to have said in his recent book *La Politique Africaine d'Houphouet Boigny* the Ivoirien leader's (read French) hostility to Nigeria's existence is very deep-rooted, and ECOWAS has only changed the arena for their combat against any form of intra-African integration independent of France. I submit this proposition for your consideration.

Chad

The third proposition is that the armed conflict in Chad, which has lasted for over sixteen years, is a continuation of the nationalist struggle against the French. In the course of this struggle spearheaded by FROLINAT, regional, tribal, clan and personality factors led to considerable fragmentation. The 'North vs. South', 'Muslim vs. Christian', 'Arab vs. Negro', terms into which this is often reduced is merely the usual crude simplifications to serve Western interests. It was the nature of Chadian economy and society and the involvements from neighboring countries which created the conditions for this fragmentation which, however, was successfully manipulated by the French to preserve their domination over that country. Even the phase of Nigeria's involvement which involved the conferences at Lagos and Kano was initiated by this French manipulation. For it was because of the suggestions of a French diplomat at the United Nations that the Obasanjo regime decided to get more involved in Chad, and its involvement never went outside the limits set by the French. In the course of all these maneuvers the latest French protégé came to be Hissene Habre, who is also supported by the U.S.A., Saudi Arabia, Sudan and Egypt. It was Libyan intervention which led to the defeat of Habre and the termination of the French strategic dominance. Given the location of Chad, right in the heart of northern Africa, and the historical and even romantic associations of the French military presence there, this defeat threatened both politically and psychologically the system of domination the French have established over Central Africa.

Nigeria's National Interest

The fourth proposition is that the collapse of the system of French domination of Central Africa is in Nigeria's national interest and therefore the Nigerian government should right now be supporting the Chad and Libyan governments in their opposition to French imperialism. Section 19 of the Constitution clearly provides that:

'The State shall promote African unity as well as the total political, economic, social and cultural liberation of Africa..'

The present Nigerian policy of defending French interests, together with governments installed and maintained by the French, is a direct violation of this section of the Constitution. The issue of the system which should replace French domination of the area should be decided by the people of the area themselves. But this right of the people of the area to self-determination is being violated by insisting on withdrawal of Libyan troops from Chad without, first and foremost, getting the French removed from the neighbouring Central African Republic, Gabon and Cameroons. This should be a pre-condition of Libyan withdrawal from Chad. Free elections should also be demanded by Nigeria not only in Chad, but also in the Central African Republic, Gabon and Cameroons after the withdrawal of French troops and facilities. I submit this proposition for your consideration.

Nigeria's Policy Towards Libya

The fifth proposition of this letter to you. Honourable Members, is that Nigeria's policy towards Libya should be to cooperate with it for achieving the goal of eliminating French domination of Central Africa and defending the right of the people of the area to determine their own destiny. This can be achieved for several obvious reasons which are now, however, hidden away. This Libyan regime of Gaddafi has been erratic and opportunistic in some of its policies in relation to Uganda and the Sudan, for example. But it is not an expansionist, pan-Islamic, and pan-Arab war-monger as the Western media tried to make it out to be. Some of the hidden facts about Libyan foreign policy is that it defied the Arab League and the Organisation of the Islamic Conference countries to support the Ethiopian government of Mengistu Haile Mariam, when Arab reactionaries, supported by the United States, were trying through Somalia and the Eritrean movements, to break up Ethiopia, using racial and religious chauvinism. The disintegration of Ethiopia under the Somalian onslaught financed by Saudi Arabia and the Gulf Emirates would have been a major disaster for the whole of Africa. On that issue, the Obasanjo regime played into the hands of Jimmy Carter and Andrew .Young and failed to support the defence of Ethiopia's territorial integrity, as the Libyan government together withAlgeria did. As for its aggressive pan-Arabism, the Libyan government is again defying the pan-Arab position and supports Iran against Iraq. Recently, the Libyan opposition to American military occupation of Saudi Arabia, particularly the recent military entrenchment of this, has led to an attempt by the Saudi government to use its control of some pan – Islamic organisations to ostracise Libya. And it is significantly Saudi Arabia and Kuwait that have been deeply involved in promoting the use of religion in political campaigns in this

63

country since the days of the N.P.C. conversion campaigns in the 1960's, which was one of the background causes of the civil war. While it is likely that pan-Islamic organisations funded by Libya operate in this country, the significance of these should be seen in the context of the far older, far more entrenched, and far more powerful organisations sponsored by Saudi Arabia and Kuwait, which after the assassination of Murtala and during the days of the Sharia debate in the Constituent Assembly almost led to violent religious conflicts in this country, and are still very active. There are also the Christian fundamentalist organisations sponsored and funded from the United States, Britain, Italy and other parts of Europe which similarly have to be considered and not covered up like the Saudi and Kuwait sponsored organisations, by a fabricated anti-Libyan hysteria.

Finally, Honourable Members, the defence of the sovereignty and territorial integrity of our country cannot be based on the purchase of armaments no matter how sophisticated or massive. The defence of these depends on the national commitment and cohesion of the common people of Nigeria, by whom alone this sovereignty can be defended and promoted. This national commitment and cohesion is inseparable from the fight for the liberation of the whole of Africa from neo-colonialism and imperialism.

Yusufu Bala Usman,
Governor's Office,
Kaduna.
Monday 26th January, 1981.

V. NO NATION! NO DESTINY!*

The Letter

Kaduna,
23rd September 1981

The Commissioner of Police,
Kaduna State Police Command, Kaduna,

Re: The Pamphlet *No Nation! No Destiny!*

With reference to the raid by thirty armed policemen on the State Headquarters of the P.R.P., at GG 15 Benin Street, Kaduna; and the arrest and interrogation, at C.I.D. headquarters, of Aminu Idris and Hassan Giwa, on the above matter.

I tried to get in touch with you yesterday, telephoning your office several times, but was told you were not available. I did get in touch with your deputy, Mr. Apapa, and informed him that this publication is produced and distributed by the National Research Directorate of the P.R.P., which I presently head, and to which all inquiries should be directed.

---

*Text of a letter written to the Commissioner of Police, Kaduna State, on 23rd September 1981; and the full text of the English translation of the Federal Radio Corporation of Nigeria, Kaduna, Hausa broadcast in the programme *Alkawnri Kaya Ne*, which I edited and which was published by the National Research Directorate of the People's Redemption Party as *No Nation' No Destiny!*. Kaduna, 1981. The title refers to the slogan of the ruling National Party of Nigeria 'One Nation! One Destiny!'

Since its contents, and current developments, make the issue of immediate significance. it is better if the position is clarified to you, in writing.

The publication *No Nation! No Destiny!* is being produced and distributed, throughout the country, by the National Research Directorate of the P.R.P. The transcription of the broadcast and its translation into English was made by Lamis Ibrahim Katsina, and the editing was done by myself.

It is being produced because it has become necessary to awaken the people of Nigeria to the serious dangers represented by the systematic campaign of tribal and sectionalist hatred being conducted by the National Party of Nigeria, whose slogan of 'One Nation! One Destiny!' has now come to mean No Nation! No Destiny!, hence the title of the publication.

This campaign of the N.P.N. is pervasive, as it is being conducted through many organs, including Federal media organs, particularly the *New Nigerian* Newspapers and the Radio Nigeria, Kaduna, for this part of the country.

As you may be aware, this campaign is being conducted not only through inciting tribal hatred but also by manipulating religious differences.

The following few examples illustrate the dangers of this campaign:

i. in the recent riots in Gboko, the lives and property of Igbo residents were threatened;
ii. your counterpart in Kano, Alhaji Sani Wali, admitted that there was a plot to attack Yorubas in Sabon-gari as part of the Friday 10th July 1981 rampage;

iii. the Niger State, right at the centre of the country, is degenerating, fast, into a cesspool of tribal and religious tensions; with the Hausa pitted against Nupe, Gbagyi, etc. by a sordid, but increasingly explosive, pattern of intrigue and manipulation;

iv. political and economic affairs between the major cities of Port Harcourt, Aba and Owerri have been reduced to the crudest level of Igbo versus others.

Nobody with a memory, or an understanding, of what happened to our country between the 1963 census and January 1970 will fold hands and allow the same old crooks to repeat what they did, and got away with, fat and prosperous.

As is clearly pointed out in the introduction to *No Nation! No Destiny!*, the current campaign of tribal and sectional hatred is being conducted by an oligarchy, which for the last thirty years has paraded itself as representing the people of the northern states, but in relation to whom it is merely a bloodsucking parasite.

Ten copies of the publication are enclosed for your use. My advice is that you direct further inquiries to the Special Adviser to the President for Information, at Ribadu Road, who is responsible for the Federal organs conducting this particularly rabid campaign, so dangerous to the unity of our country, which the publication brought out.

Contact me for any more information you may need on the matter.

Yusufu Bala Usman
Governor's Office,
Kaduna.

The Broadcast

(English Translation of the text of a Federal Radio Nigeria, Kaduna, Hausa programme, broadcast for four days: Friday, 7th August 1981- Monday 10th August 1981.)

I do not have the intention of pursuing this Balarabe Musa matter. What I would like to talk about today is a completely different matter; a matter even mentioned to one of you.

It is on something that took place in Lagos. This is at a large government estate popularly known as 'One Thousand and Four'.

At this place there were several people. At first there were only six people. They were making a lot of noise on the political goings-on in the country. The six people were members of certain Legislature. One of the six is odd among them, in the sense that the other five were legislators from Plateau State. That state which had recently taken up the invitation of joining the so-called progressive states, who parade themselves as people to bring changes in this country. Shanshani said, because of some strong reasons the real names of these people will not be mentioned. But let us assume they bore these names. Among them were Damen, Dapshik, Lavar, Isaac and the fifth Kantiyok. The odd man among them was from Sokoto State. And Sokoto is the cradle of Hausa-Fulani hegemony. If one doesn't like this name, then we can call it by the name the *Nigerian Standard* gave it. That is Sokoto, the birth-place of Sardauna the tyrant, the oppressor.- Let us assume the Sokoto man to be called Tahiru, as Shanshani said. "I really pity this man Tahiru," Shanshani said. He was about to get out of this large government building. At that moment a young and handsome man entered. He was also from the northern states, and from his looks he must be from Fulani or Hausa extraction or both. Shanshani said he estimated the age of this man to be just above forty. There were two vacant seats and he went there. Before he sat, he looked at the six people who were sitting. He greeted them. Only Tahiru answered him. In any case he ignored that and took his seat.

Shanshani said, "let us assume the name of this man was Abubakar;" Abubakar sat there quietly as if he was not aware of the presence of those other people. After three minutes he became worked up with all they were saying. He joined the discussion of those people. This was how it went on. Abubakar said to those legislators let me tell you one thing. "You who are saying all sorts of terrible things about Hausas and Fulanis, must face the fact that you are a minority. Are you aware of that?" They were brought to their senses by this, because it occurred to them so terribly, like the prophecy of doom. They answered "yes". "Besides this, you can look at any place in the world and you will confirm this. That in any country where there are minorities and majorities, it is always the majorities ruling over the minorities. Are you aware of this?" Here they also answered "yes". Then he said, "even if it may so happen that you have a situation where the minorities rule the majorities you will find that they can only do it with the unconditional support of the majorities". They did not argue this fact, Abubakar pointed out. So they said "yes". Abubakar said he was going to say something and challenged any of them to take him to task. He said that throughout the history of the former North, there never existed the rule of despotism and oppression by the majority over the minority. Because there never was a case where a Hausa got something and the other not getting it because he was a non-Hausa minority. "If one is sincere and knows what he is doing he will confirm what I said. Since this is the fact, I don't see any reason why you should be sharpening your axe against we Hausas. Because you don't have any ground!" Abubakar said. "What is more, in the present Nigerian reality whether you like it or not, when political matters arise you must align with either the Hausas, the Yorubas or with the Inyamurai (the Igbos). That is the fact: whether you like it or not, you must align with either of the three major tribes if you want to survive. And even at that, you must know the superior among them. So let me tell the bitter thing you don't like to hear. In one hundred years to come in this country, anybody who said he will rule this country without the support of the Hausas and the Fulani, such a man is fooling himself. I repeat, he is fooling himself. He is living in fool's paradise! It is your business to cooperate with any of the two other majority tribes", Abubakar concluded. "But what you must bear in mind is that none of the other two will solve your problems. Because they too must seek the support of the Hausas and Fulanis you are hating, and teaching others to hate. If somebody is denying this fact, we should go and ask the Yorubas or the Inyamurai; they know this. Again there is one thing I will point to you, we never worry our heads for the fact that you hate us. The fact is we pity you! Because at this moment you are nothing! If one looks at the prevailing situation, whether you exist or you don't exist, things will go on. Plateau State can go on preaching to its people to hate Hausa and Fulani hegemony for the next one hundred years to come. It amounts to nothing!"

"And here I am not talking about N.P.N. No, you can take any political party, N.P.P., G.N.P.P., U.P.N. or P.R.P., wherever you go, you must come back to cooperate with the Hausa and Fulani. The two which constitute the largest majority in this country. You better start purging yourselves right now, re-orient your thinking and get to know your fool- ishness in hating the Hausas and the Fulani and teaching that to your people. This was never our headache. From all indi- cations you are enjoying what you are doing. But to us you are wasting your time."

"In any case, may Allah preserve us; the day the account will be squared. You are entertaining yourselves in the pleasure of turning your press to be the organ of defam- ing the name of the Hausas, their leaders, abusing them and their traditional royalty and their cultural heritage. We wish you good luck. But as I said, the day of settling accounts will definitely come. You, more than anybody know that the Hausas you have been abusing are not fools. You are hating the Hausas on three main reasons. The first being the ques- tion of religious differences, something which you and your leaders made worse. The second, you are still nursing your grief over what happened to you after the assassination of Murtala. The third reason why you are stilt blaming the Hausas, to the extent that you are feeling you have a score to settle with them is this. That since the inception of the civilian rule even before the talk of an accord between the N.P.N. and N.P.P started, it was your government and your people who had been campaigning to the people that all should cooperate with the Federal Government. And. there should be tolerance.

That didn't go that far before you unmasked your evil motive. You clearly showed that you and your government do not care whether the Shagari administration succeeds or not. It was all the same to you. You shamelessly came out to show the world that the only thing you were concerned with was the return of Yakubu Gowon to Nigeria. You became deeply emotional on this. This was also the case with the Inyamurai and their two N.P.P. governments. They knew their objective, that was why they entered into an accord with the N.P.N. An accord which is now dead. Their purpose of getting into this accord was to have the rebel leader Ojukwu to return home. What is more, your leaders refused to see the true picture of the issue. They turned the issue of letting Ojukwu to come home into politics. They went to the extent of attempting to tarnish the good image of the President on this. Or at least to put the blame on him. You were doing all these with the full knowledge that these men's crimes were against the nation. Crimes which even though they differ, they had been committed against the State."

"What happened in the end? Since the time President Shagari ignored you on this matter. Since the time he came out clearly to tell your leaders that he would not allow himself to be dragged into this matter with the purpose of tarnishing his image, since tribalism had taken much of your sense to the extent of agitating your students to take placards making noise in the streets on something not political. Since the time Shagari told you to go and join those who turn the issue into politics, it was since then that you who call yourselves people of Plateau State, together with the Inyamurai, who are in the N.P.P., created another reason to hate the Hausas. You broke the accord between N.P.P. and

N.P.N. An accord which has no meaning under the present system, in any case. And in your state you started many things showing your hatred to Hausas and Fulanis. This is done with the full support of those two mavericks of Kaduna and Kano, who do this in the name of revolution. People who in reality are nothing more than rebels, relatives of Satan, who enjoy being prodigal sons."

"And here is one other thing. Are you aware of the fact that in all these it is you who will suffer most? Not far. In your state a formidable dilemma is facing you. Just because some people have come out to ask for Middle Belt State. Something which is quite constitutional. By,looking at the way you handle the question of Middle Belt State anyone can see you don't like the Hausas or Fulanis. What you have done has shown clearly that you more than anyone else feel threatened, that you cannot bear political tolerance. You refuse to face the fact. Or you just ignore it. You are so confused that you don't realise the fact that you were the very people who put this trap of Middle Belt State. Instead of realising your mistakes, you turn round to blame your political opponents. You refuse to see the agitations of more states being waged by the people of Anambra and Imo States, the states which constitute the birth place of that old Owelle. The states where also Jim Nwobodo and Sam Mbakwe, your new godfathers, live."

"Not only this. Look at the matter clearly to see the limit of your senses and intelligence. The Secretary of your party Dr. Alex Fom had said there was need for creating two more states from Plateau State. And you supported his decision. But it is Danladi Yakubu you want to crucify because he said he supports the creation of Middle Belt State,

73

because he is a Hausa and a Fulani. If this is not clear sign of hatred towards someone not of your tribe what is it? You explain this behaviour to me!"

Shanshani said from here he does not have to tell us what happened next. I don't need to tell you that these people from Plateau State kept quiet as if they had been drowned. They had met their equal.

Eventually, as Shanshani said, I later found something about this Abubakar who had said all this. The fact is, he is not a politician, and is not a civil servant. As to Western education, he has much of it. Because he has two degrees. About ten years ago a body of the United Nations gave him a very big post because of the exceptional performance he showed when he was a student in America. But because of his nationalism he turned down the offer. That he preferred to come back and serve his country Nigeria. Good evening. Now listeners, all I will say is, till we meet next week.

VI. THE MANIPULATION OF RELIGION IN NIGERIA TODAY: THE DOMESTIC AND FOREIGN CONNECTIONS*

A series of violent demonstrations, riots and civil uprisings in this country in the last two years, have forcefully made many Nigerians come face-to-face with the harsh reality that religion is being systematically manipulated, by some forces, for specific purposes which are clearly opposed to the unity of the people of this country.

Violent clashes connected ostensibly, or actually, with religion are not unknown in this country. These have occurred over the activity of preachers; the sitting, control or connections of churches, mosques and even schools; and over other matters connected with religious authority and religious organisations, in all parts of the country.

The Significance of the Recent Religious Violence

What is distinctive, however, about the recent violent occurrences connected with religion are their scale, intensity, and symmetry.

The Maitatsine Uprising in Kano City from 18th December, 1980 to 29th December, 1980, led, according to official figures, to the killing of 4,177 (four thousand, one hundred and seventy-seven) civilians! Even if the actual figures of those killed is not much higher, this amounts to a massive slaughter of human beings, by whatever standard. Since the end of the crisis and civil war of 1966-1970, this

---

*Published in the *Sunday Triumph*, 14th November, 1982 and 21st **November, 1982, and** *The Nigerian Standard,* 11th and 12th **November, 1982.**

75

country has not gone through the agony of violence of such a scale and intensity, anywhere.

The Maitatsine Uprising also involved the extensive destruction of houses, shops and other property, and the disruption of normal life in the country's third largest city, and an important economic centre.

The recent Bulunkutu Uprising in Maiduguri from Tuesday, 26th October, 1982 to Saturday, 30th October, 1982 has also led to the killing of over 400 persons according to newspaper reports. There was also large-scale destruction of houses, hotels and other property and the disruption of normal life in the country's north-eastern metropolis, for several days.

The riots in Kaduna, from Friday 29th October, 1982 to Sunday 31st October, 1982, led to the killing of over 40 persons, according to official reports. Destruction of houses and other property also took place.

The violent demonstration in Sabon Gari Kano by the Muslim Students Society on Saturday, 30th October, 1982, involved killing on a much smaller scale. Only two people were killed, according to newspaper reports. But the great significance of this incident is that it involves, for the first time, the calculated destruction and burning of Christian churches in what seems to be a violent assertion of the 'Islam only' slogan painted all over the streets of Zaria in an aggressive, demonstration by the Muslim Students Society in 1980.

The attack on, and destruction of, Christian churches in Sabon Garin Kano, marks the highest, and most dangerous, point this systematic manipulation of religion has yet reached in its opposition to the unity of the people of this country. The incident also enables us to see more clearly the purposes and

76

direction of this campaign of manipulation built around religion.

What Exactly is a Religious Fanatic?

In the face of this calculated and violent threat to the unity of the people of this country, the usual labelling of those organising and executing these violent acts merely as 'religious fanatics', 'Islamic fundamentalists', 'Muslim extremists', is as obscure and evasive as it is unsatisfactory.

To say that Maitatsine and his gang, or the members of the Muslim Students Society responsible for these violent acts are 'religious fanatics' and 'Islamic fundamentalists' is to say very little. There are people who are labelled 'religious fanatics' and 'Islamic fundamentalists' fighting right now on both sides of the battle lines along the Iran-Iraqi border. There are people who are labelled 'religious fanatics' and 'Islamic fundamentalists' fighting for, and against, the Israeli occupation forces in southern Lebanon and Beirut. To say that some person, or organisation, is a 'religious fanatic' and 'Islamic fundamentalist' in contemporary Nigeria, and in other parts of the world, is to say virtually nothing about them. In fact it often gives the misleading impression that religion has something to do with their actions, beyond the level of very superficial rituals and symbolism.

A central question, in relating these violent actions religion and the society, which is often evaded, is, what are they actually *fanatical* about? What beliefs, values, practice's, in contemporary Nigeria, are they specifically, fanatically opposed to, or in support of? What exactly is it in the Islamic faith and practice in the contemporary world that they regard as so fundamental as to determine all their actions to totally and exclusively?

Who Was Maitatsine?

Over Maitatsine's followers, some people may answer this question by saying that they are fanatical about, and regard as fundamental, their belief that Maitatsine was a 'prophet'. But this answer raises more questions than it answers. Who exactly was this Muhammadu Marwa, *alias* Muhammadu Arab, *alias* Muhammadu Mai Tabsiri, *alias* Muhammadu Marwa Darka, *alias* Muhammadu Allah Ta Tsine, *alias* Maitatsine? What were his beliefs? Where did he stand on the major theological, social, political and cultural issues of his day? What social and political forces did he embody, serve, symbolise and represent?

It is very significant that this *Report of the Kono Disturbances Tribunal of Inquiry*, a tribunal set up by President Shehu Shagari, under the Chairmanship of Justice Anthony Antagolu, never brought out exactly the identity, background, beliefs and connections of Maitatsine and his followers. The report never told us even what exactly they were fanatical about. This is in spite of the fact that they had as a member a learned Islamic scholar, preacher and jurist, in the person of Alhaji Ustaz Younus Abdullahi, a qadi of Kwara State and a leading member of the Jama'atu Nasrul Islam.

In fact, on the two occasions when the Aniagolu Tribunal touched upon Maitatsine's beliefs and outlook, it quickly contradicted itself, leaving the reader of their report in complete confusion.

Let us take the first occasion. On page 25 of the report, the Tribunal states that:

"He (Maitatsine) totally condemned the main principles of Islam as laid down by the Qur'an and the Sunnat. He condemned the Holy Qur'an and denounced the prophethood of Prophet Mohammed. At a stage he declared himself a prophet. By this self-declaration of prophethood the former hostile religious preacher assumed a new role of *Annabi* meaning 'prophet' and he caused his students in Kano and other places to believe in his new mission."

But on the very next page of the report, that is page 26, the Tribunal directly contradicted this. It states:

"Maitatsine ostensibly declared his prophethood to his followers sometimes in 1979 but deceitfully professed to the outside world that he was propagating Islam. His doctrine could be confirmed in Exhibit 83, appendix 2 particularly paragraph 3 which reads:

These preacher's doctrines are reported as follows:

a. That anyone who rides on a bicycle or a motorcycle is a pagan.

b. That any Muslim, who includes *Allahu Akbar* in his prayers, reads the *Tahita* or says *Atahiyat Rak Ataine* after prayer is a pagan.

c. That any Muslim who reads any book besides the Koran is a pagan.' "

How can Maitatsine be said to condemn the Koran, as part of his doctrine, on page .25, and then on page 26 be said to approve its reading, as the only book a Muslim is allowed to read? The Tribunal leaves the reader in complete confusion as to what exactly Maitatsine stood for even on this very basic issue in the faith of a Muslim.

The second example of this type of confusion over what Maitatsine stood for comes in a reference to his ideas as they relate to society. On page 208 of the report, the Tribunal states that:

> "The profanation of the venerable name and authority of the Holy Prophet which the Maitatsine episode exemplified includes, in that case, the propagation of a neo-socialist religious doctrine regarding worldly possessions which was completely strange to Islam..."

How can a preacher who condemns the riding of a bicycle or a motor-cycle, but, apparently, does not condemn the riding of a saloon car be regarded as 'neo-socialist' in contemporary Kano, or for that matter, anywhere in the world today?

But the confusion over Maitatsine's 'neo-socialism' is deepened, and the reader left bewildered, by the evidence referred to by the Tribunal regarding Maitatsine's relations with his students, cited on pages 189-190 of the report. The Tribunal states that:

> "Many mallams preach and teach the Koran more as a means of livelihood than anything else. The number of *almajirai* (students) a mallam had would determine his income... We were satisfied that the students of Maitatsine had, provided him with means of livelihood. His wife Zeinab told the Tribunal that her husband was getting money as alms at the average of two hundred Naira

(₦200.00) daily. One of the fanatics, Garba Hamza (witness no.9), stated that whenever they had money they used 'to give some to Maitatsine. With the amount of money Muhammadu Marwa was getting daily he would never have thought of himself doing without these students... This aspect of Marwa's sources of finance was one of the motivating factors which initially urged him to organise students and preach, particularly in Kano, hitherto regarded as the most affluent Muslim society in Nigeria."

It is impossible to see anything even near 'neo-socialist', either in the 'doctrines' of Maitatsine, as identified by the Tribunal on page 26, or in his relationship with his students, as represented by the Tribunal and quoted above. In the end we are left in complete confusion as to what exactly Maitatsine stood for. This confusion, created deliberately or not, by a series of glaring contradictions, may have been somewhat cleared if the Tribunal had listed in the report the name of Maitatsine's powerful patrons, which according to news media reports was supplied to it by the Nigerian Security Organisation during its sitting in Kano. Instead of doing this, the Tribunal only stated on page 81 of its report that it is convinced that it was impossible for Maitatsine to operate as he did without such patrons.

The Myth of the Aliens

Another area of glaring contradiction between differ-ent parts of the Aniagolu Report is over the national and social composition of Maitatsine's followers and even something as elementary as the exact nationality of Maitatsine himself.

On page 131 of the report the Tribunal states that only 20% of his followers arrested by the police were from neighboring West African countries. In fact out of these 185 so-called 'aliens', a total of 162, that is about 90% of the aliens, are said to be from the Niger Republic, and almost all of whom had no travel document whatsoever. Citizens of Niger Republic cannot, in most cases, be easily distinguished from Nigerian citizens of Kano State origin. The number from Niger Republic is therefore suspect in light of the obvious anxiety of the Tribunal to sell the myth that the whole Maitatsine Uprising was due to the influx of fanatical aliens into Nigeria.

But even if we accept the Tribunal's estimate that 20% of the followers of Maitatsine arrested were aliens, on what basis can the Tribunal make the assertion in page 134 that:

"...a substantial part of his followers who numbered ten thousand fanatics at the time when the insurrection was crushed and who were subsequently identified (were) citizens of Niger Republic, Chad, Cameroon, Mali and Upper Volta."

When were these 'ten thousand fanatics' identified as substantially coming from outside Nigeria? The only basis the Tribunal had for knowing about the national composition of Maitatsine's followers is the report on those arrested by the police who totalled 954, out of which even according to the Tribunal itself only 20% were not from Nigeria. How can 20% be regarded as a 'substantial' proportion?

As for the nationality of Maitatsine himself, no evidence is cited by the Tribunal beyond that one of his five aliases is 'Marwa' to support their assumption that he is a Camerounian. During the four month sitting of the Tribunal no attempt was made to have this assumption checked with the Nigeria Police, Special Branch records now with the N.S.O., and the Nigerian Prison Services, to find out if when he was jailed under security detention in Makurdi Prison in July 1973 he was recorded as a Nigerian or as a Camerounian. No attempt was also made to check the question of his nationality with the government of Cameroun if the Nigerian records are silent.

Since no attempt was made to conduct these elementary investigations by the Tribunal, during all of its four months sitting, it can also be assumed feasible that the name 'Marwa', the main basis on which his so-called Camerounian nationality rests, is only a shortened version of the known Nigerian Muslim name of 'Muhammadu Marwana'. The Tribunal did not investigate this possibility, because it was anxious to start an aliens myth to cover up the real nature of the Maitatsine gang.

As for his alleged deportation in 1962, by the Emir of Kano, Sanusi, this is even regarded with suspicion by the Tribunal, which on page 26 referred to

"the deportation order purportedly served on him by the former Emir, Alhaji Muhammadu Sanusi in1962..."

In fact the Tribunal had evidence from its exhibit 39, in the form of local government tax receipts issued to Maitatsine by the Kano Municipal Local Government, for all the fifteen years from 1963 to 1978, to question this 'deportation' story; unless he was only 'deported' for one year! In any case, the lawyers of the Tribunal, and the Chairman himself, a Justice of the Supreme Court of Nigeria, know very well that in 1962 no emir or even regional government, had the power to deport any alien from Nigeria. Only the Federal Government had such power. The Tribunal did not closely question the deportation story because of its anxiety to "establish an alien myth.

Serious suspicions about the Tribunal's integrity are raised by their evasiveness over exhibits no. 13 and 13, namely the Nigerian passport and vaccination certificate of Maitatsine, and exhibit no. 14, the completed Nigerian passport application form for Maitatsine and his son. The Tribunal evades the significance of these important pieces of evidence and on page -130 asserts that Maitatsine's Camerounian nationality is not in doubt. Surely there is no better, legal, way of establishing Maitatsine's nationality than by enquiring into his claim that he is a Nigerian citizen from the Mubi area of Gongola State, by investigating the records about his Nigerian passport at the Passport Office and the village in Nigeria he claims to come from. The Tribunal refused to do all these. Many months later the *Sunday New Nigerian sent* a reporter to Maroua in the Cameroons in search of Maitatsine's home background. If the *Sunday New Nigerian,* and those directing it in this cover-up exercise, were serious about finding Maitatsine's home, they should have started with records in the Passport Office in Lagos and with the person who officially sponsored Maitatsine to get the passport.

That in fact Maitatsine was a Nigerian citizen, and not a Camerounian, is further confirmed by the fact that after his arrest with five of his followers on 16th July, 1973, in Kano, for 'breach of the peace', he was not deported, as would most likely have happened to an alien not convicted by a court to serve a term of imprisonment. Instead he was jailed in Makurdi prison under the detention decrees of the military regime.

For how long he stayed, or even whether he stayed in the prison at all, is in doubt, because his tax receipts from Kano Municipal Local Government cover all the fifteen years from 1963 to 1978. Persons detained under the Armed Forces and Police Detention Decree, as police record indicates he was, did not pay tax! This is a major issue regarding the background of Maitatsine which this Tribunal of Inquiry did not care to inquire into.

Reliable information about Maitatsine before 1980 is so sketchy, and where it is specific, so contradictory, that one can legitimately wonder whether he actually existed; and if he existed, whether he had anything to do with the uprising.

A document cited in *The Views and Comments of the Kano State Government on the Report of the Kano Disturbances Tribunal of Inquiry*, throws some light on who Maitatsine was. Although this document was available to the Tribunal, it did not pursue the line of inquiry it opened up about Maitatsine's patrons and connections.

This document is letter No. 057/346 of 13th September, 1975, from Commissioner of Police, Kano, to Commissioner of Police (Special Branch), Lagos, reporting what it calls a near showdown at Ringim, in Kano State. In this incident, on 12th August, 1975, Maitatsine was sponsored by Alhaji Uba Ringim, a powerful Kano tycoon and former member of the N.P.C. in the Northern House of Assembly, and presently a leading member of the National Party of Nigeria, in a confrontation with a group led by Mallam Ila

Ringim, a well-known N.E.P.U. hero of the area. Maitatsine was given this powerful man's protection and got off easily, while Mallam Ila Ringim was hauled before the police and warned to keep the peace.

Why was this lead not followed by the Tribunal to enquire into the patrons and connections of Maitatsine and his activities before and after this Ringom incident of 12th August, 1975? But this very serious lapse in the conduct of the inquiry further shows up the attempt to cover up the real nature of Maitatsine's group with the alien myth, as shaky as it is shoddy and unpatriotic.

In the light of this, Alhaji Umaru Dikko, the Minister of Transport's claim reported in the *Sunday New Nigerian* of 7th November, 1982, that there is no evidence to connect Maitatsine's followers released by President Shagari on 1st October, 1982, with the recent violence, makes sense. There is precisely no evidence for anyone to check this, independently of the Federal Government, because the Tribunal did not provide in its report details on, at least, the names, place of origin, age, occupation, and parents of the over 900 followers of Maitatsine arrested and now released. Only the Federal Government agencies can, if they wish, release this – if they even compiled them!

The Meaning of 'Islam Only'

If a Tribunal of Inquiry established by the President, and chaired by a Justice of the Supreme Court of Nigeria, with a Senior Advocate of Nigeria (SAN) as its counsel, could sit for over four months, with all the powerful resources of the Federal Government at its disposal and still leave us in such confusion over the nature of Maitatsine and his gang, and even their nationality, beyond the label of 'religious fanatics', it is not surprising that the various official and newspaper reports on the Muslim Students Society do not go beyond such labelling, which obscures more than it explains. Although the Muslim Students Society seems to have started to practicalise its slogan of 'Islam only' by burning churches in Sabon Gari, Kano, none of the reports on its nature and activity that I have come across go into the type of Islamic society and state the members of this society want built in Nigeria; and into whether they want this established for all the people of Nigeria or only for Muslims. The question of whether the Islamic government they want is closer to that of the Saudi dynasty; or the Islamic Republics of Pakistan or of Iran or to the Libyan Jamhiriyya, is never even raised, in spite of the wide range between them at the theological, social, political and cultural levels.

The Deliberate Generation of Fear

The result of all this confusion and lack of sound and coherent information is that instead of the Nigerian public seeing these 'religious fanatics' with their social and political substance and meaning., in the context of contemporary Nigerian society, they are reduced to dark irrational forces. These can only generate fear, foreboding, and insecurity among other Muslims, and particularly among non-Muslim Nigerians. This blind fear of the unknown, of something irrational, which one cannot understand, but which may, at any time, violently strike out against one's life and property, only loosens the fibres of the threads which are forging the unity of the people of this country. It also undermines popular participation in democratic activity across the various nationalities of the country, which alone can bring the common people to realise their common interests over and above any geographical, ethnic, religious or cultural differences. The deliberate generation of such fear therefore has specific, concrete, and far-reaching political consequences.

Given the seriousness of these consequences; given the official' Federal Government attempt to blame these violent outbreaks on aliens, since the Aniagolu Tribunal; given the speed with which a wall of evasion and deception is being built officially to cover up the campaign of the manipulation of religion behind these outbreaks; it is necessary to continue exposing it, in order" to generate greater public awareness and public capacity to organise and defend our basic democratic and civic rights and the unity of our country. This is the purpose of this essay.

The Pattern of the Manipulation

In a public lecture at the Kongo Campus of the Ahmadu Bello University on Monday, 28th November, 1977 on the subject of 'The Manipulation of Religion in Nigeria Today: Its Social and Political Basis', I tried to sketch out the pattern this manipulation had taken from the assassination of Murtala Muhammed on Friday, 13th February, 1976, to the Shari'a campaign then beginning to reach its peak in the Constituent Assembly,

In fact, the beginnings of the current phase of the manipulation of religion in Nigeria today go back to the period of the decay and decline of the Gowon regime in the early 1970's.

The civil war had, generally, led to the open and direct political utilisation of religion and religious institutions, both Muslim and Christian, to support the cause of the unity of Nigeria, against the very powerful pro-secessionist propaganda from many Christian missionary organisations from Western Europe, America and many parts of Africa. There was no question of manipulation in this case, as the purpose of the campaign was not hidden from the people of Nigeria and other parts of the world. The purpose was openly stated to be the preservation of Nigeria as one country, and it was successfully achieved with the defeat of the Biafran secessionist movement in 1970.

After the defeat of secession the Gowon regime sunk further into a morass of corruption, waste, incompetence, and repression. This led to its increasing political isolation and its attempts to mobilise support through various means, including around Yakubu Gowon's image of 'muscular Christianity', as the orator of the University of Cambridge evoked, when Gowon was being awarded an honorary doctorate degree of that University in June 1975. This image of Gowon as a devout Christian is an extension of the political use of his 'minority' background whose assertion, the regime's policy of forging national unity came to be reduced to.

The opposition to the Gowon regime from the section of the northern oligarchy with powerful financial and political ambitions he could not fulfill, although they were influential and well-placed in the regime, took an increasingly religious tone. The former 'good northerner' from Barewa College, Zaria, soon came to be 'the Christian missionary's boy' from Pankshin. No matter how many meetings of the Barewa Old Boys Association Gowon went to, or emirs he paid courtesy calls upon, this section of the northern oligarchy relentlessly pursued this change of his political image. Their systematic use of the powerful radio, television and newspaper organs set up in Kaduna by the former Northern Regional Government, then under the Interim Common Services Agency (ICSA) enabled them to widely propagate their views.

It was in this context that Alhaji Abubakar Gummi, the former Grand Khadi of the Northern Region and former adviser in Islamic and Arab affairs to the late Premier of the Northern Region, Sir Ahmadu Bello, the Sardauna of Sokoto, emerged as an important public figure once again.

This time he emerged as a critic of the corruption and moral decadence of a Nigerian regime, instead of as a supporter, providing legal and religious cover for these, as he was doing for the N.P.C, regime. He made effective use of his sermons and commentaries on his translations of the Holy Koran to fluently criticise the low moral standards of Nigerian society and almost explicitly presented the Gowon regime as anti-Islamic in its nature. The ICSA media organs in Kaduna, particularly the radio were used to carry his sermons, comments and statements very powerfully and widely.

This posture towards the Gowon regime, of Alhaji Abubakar Gummi, gave him considerable credibility in a period when the corruption and arrogance of Gowon's military governors and top officials was so nauseating. But it also further justified the mobilisation of support for Gowon by his closest supporters in the regime on a Christian platform; and together the conditions were created for the rapid acceleration of the manipulation of religion, with the assassination of Murtala Muhammed on Friday, 13th February, 1976.

When Murtala was assassinated on the morning of that Friday, the Muslim World League, an agency of the Saudi Arabian Government, with which Alhaji Abubakar Gummi is closely associated, sent a message to Nigerian Muslims for the loss of a Muslim leader, which was reported in the *New Nigerian* of 4th March, 1976. This message was clearly intended to cause violent religious conflict between Muslims and Christians over the death of Murtala. The overwhelming and popular sense of national loss and grief in all parts of the country, however, completely made this impossible.

This message of condolence from the Muslim World League seems to have been part of an Anglo-American operation, which included the assassination of Murtata, to wreck the strong nationalist and pan-Africanist momentum and commitment which Nigeria had gained in only about one hundred and ninety-six days of Murtala's regime. This was clearly demonstrated in the popular domestic support for, and decisiveness, of the policy of support for the MPLA in Angola, in open and direct opposition and defiance of America, which was then getting Saudi Arabia to supplement its support to its puppet Angolan movements by the Saudis channeling funds to the F.N.L.A. of Holden Roberto. A B.B.C. broadcast immediately after Murtala's assassination, reporting that communal violence had broken out in Nigeria because of it, seems to have been part of this Anglo-American operation against Nigeria, with direct Saudi Arabian collaboration, through the Muslim World League. The manipulation of religion continued over the investigation, trials and execution of those involved in the assassination and the attempted coup. It merged with the political maneuvering over the new constitution and the 1979 elections to reach a peak in the Shari'a campaign inside and outside the Constituent Assembly in 1977-78.

The Shari'a Campaign

This campaign, under the cover of debating the provisions of the draft constitution with regards to a Federal Shari'a Court of Appeal, has already been touched upon in the earlier lecture referred to above.

Here, it is perhaps sufficient to show how the political and psychological conditions for the sustenance and violent operations of gangs like Maitatsine's and the bands of the Muslim Students Society were deliberately prepared. For even, as the Aniagolu Tribunal admitted on pages 180, 209-214 of their report, Maitatsine's gang flourished in the psychological atmosphere created by a great deal of stress and tension over religion.

The Shari'a campaign involved virulent and inciting attacks on aspects of Islam and Christianity over the radio, television and newspapers. The *New Nigerian* newspaper articles by Ibraheem Suleiman of the Centre of Islamic Legal Studies, of Ahmadu Bello University, and the responses by reverend fathers and others, in the *Nigerian Standard* were perhaps the most bigoted and provocative examples of this systematic campaign of manipulating religion.

But the most irresponsible examples are some of the speeches in the Constituent Assembly, where after taking an oath on the Koran or the Bible to faithfully serve Nigeria, some of the members set out to generate the psychological atmosphere for destroying it.

Not surprisingly it was Alhaji Turi Muhammadu, then Managing Director of *New Nigerian* Newspapers, Kaduna, belonging to the section of the northern oligarchy promoting Alhaji Abubakar Gummi, who started evoking images of violence against Muslims in the Constituent Assembly debates.

On Tuesday, 1st November, 1977, Alhaji Turi Muhammadu said on the issue of whether the provision of a Federal Shari'a Court of Appeal should be left in the draft constitution, that:

"The other person said the whole provision of the Shari'a should be wiped out. If that is his idea, then all the Muslims in the country should be wiped out too."

The debate on the Shari'a came to dominate the Constituent Assembly so much that the whole political, social and psychological atmosphere in the country became highly charged with religious animosities. In the end the Obasanjo regime had to terminate the proceedings of the Assembly unceremoniously, after several warnings to the members had failed to bring them to take a more patriotic stand on this and other issues. Their postures and rhetoric for and against Shari'a brought the country to the brink of religious riots.

One of the more interesting of the fiery speeches stoking up this Shari'a campaign is one by Alhaji Umaru Dikko, present Minister of Transport and one of the most powerful members of the Shagari regime, with clearly presidential ambitions. Alhaji Umaru Dikko's remarks were as false and misleading as they were irresponsible. On Monday, 14th November, 1977, Alhaji Umaru Dikko stated:

> "Moslems in Nigeria, Mr. Chairman, have suffered so much discrimination. I shall prove this, Mr. Chairman. Some of us were witnesses in the days of colonial era in this country when a Moslem purely on account of religion was not admitted in the State House... regardless of the way you feel about us, you should give us the right to worship our God in the way we understand..."

Both Turi Muhammadu and Umaru Dikko knew very well that there was no question of 'wiping out' Muslims or of denying them the right to be Muslims. They took this posture and evoked these alarming images of violence and suppression in order to create a religious constituency which they believe they and their type can mobilise to defend their privileges and perpetuate the present system where they sit on top, serving Western business interests in exploiting the people and resources of Nigeria. Religion, Shari'a, culture, etc. is a convenient cover.

In my earlier lecture on this subject referred to above, I tried to explain the social and political bases of this manipulation of religion in the political economy of Nigeria. Since in the last five years the Turi Muhammadus and the Umaru Dikkos, the Mvendega Jibos and Paul Unongos, have only further confirmed this explanation in practice, I shall only quote what I said then:

> "...the intermediary bourgeois cannot appear as what he really is in the political economy of Nigeria. He has to find a cover. He cannot claim political leadership openly on the grounds that he

is, or wants to be, an exporter-importer, a contractor, commission-agent, share-holder, rentier or rich bureaucrat. He has to take cover as a Muslim or Christian. He has to take cover as an Ibo, Hausa, Idoma, or Efik. He has to take on disguises. He has to posture as a 'majority' or *a* 'minority'. The manipulation of religion in Nigeria today is essentially a means of creating the context for this fancy dress ball, for this charade of disguises . . . (It) is to enable this class to cover themselves with religious... disguises in order to further entrench division among our people, slow down their awakening, at any cost; even the unity of our country for which so much has been sacrificed."

The Saudi Connection

The domestic pattern of the manipulation of religion in Nigeria today sketched out above can only be understood in the context of how American imperialism has been systematically using its two major agents in the Middle East, namely the governments of Saudi Arabia and that of Israel, to monitor and utilise this type of activity, even where it is not responsible for initiating it.

This understanding cannot be achieved unless we see clearly the way these two, apparently opposed, instruments of American imperialist strategy, work for a common purpose in manipulating religion in Africa. The degree of the subservience of the Saudi Arabian government to America is not often understood in this country because of the Arab dresses and Islamic rhetoric of the rulers and their spokesmen and agents, This subservience extends to the economic base of the Saudi ruling class being service to American oil companies; and even to the actual stationing of American troops on Saudi soil and nearby ships and bases, solely to protect this regime.

Here I will only cite two examples to illustrate this degree of subservience and how Islam and Islamic organisations are used to entrench and implement American policies by the Saudi Arabian government. The Muslim World League one of the oldest and most prestigious of the many international Islamic organisations controlled by the Saudi regime. Its monthly journal is widely read by Muslim intellectuals and students all over the world. Its funding extends to all spheres and to all parts of the world where Muslims live. It appears to stand for the independent, and creative role for Muslims and for Islamic civilisation in the contemporary world.

In its obituary for the late King Khalid who died on 13th June, 1982, the June 1982 edition of the journal (vol. 9 no. 8) had this to say in praise of the late king:

"King Khalid was active in Arab and international affairs from the beginning. As a ruler of the world's biggest oil exporting country he was instrumental in holding back rising oil prices." (p. 6)

The obituary did not go further to state, or even indicate, how this particular role for a Muslim king can be said to be an achievement, outside the view that he and his government exist to serve American imperialism, which is bitterly opposed to rising oil prices, and which has now successfully used Saudi Arabia to prevent them rising, while the price of exports to the oil-producing countries continues to rise, and the profits of their companies soar. This brief quotation brings out more clearly the role of Saudi Arabia and of its organs like the Muslim World League, more than pages of analyses.

I will now cite the second example, which comes, from an item in the same journal of the Muslim World League, but this time on page 31, of vol. 9 no. 7 of May 1982. This is in connection with the role Saudi Arabia plays, using its Islamic status and connections, to promote American policy in Africa.

As part of the campaign to topple Muammar Ghaddafi, the Libyan leader, or at least curb and destroy his anti-imperialist influence in Africa, the American government of Ronald Reagan launched a propaganda offensive against him in 1981. This culminated in their successfully sabotaging the O.A.U. Tripoli summit and thus has prevented Ghaddafi from assuming the chairmanship of the O.A.U., up to today.

The Saudi role in this, in influencing many African regimes to support American policy and in financially and diplomatically sustaining King Hassan's invasion of the Saharawi Republic is well known. What is however not so well-known is that in the last stages of the campaign to sabotage the Tripoli summit of the O.A.U., the Saudi regime brought forward some of its heaviest artillery and directed this against Ghaddafi. A meeting of the Grand Council of the Ulema of Saudi Arabia was convened on Saturday, 6th 1982, at Riyadh. The meeting issued an edict for all Muslims in the world which grandly declared:

"...he (Ghaddafi) is considered *a* non-Muslim, an atheist, who in addition to his dictatorship, oppressive policies and false allegations against the people commits something that does not behave sane and respectable people... Ghaddafi now

97

surpasses all others and has vowed to serve evil and spread chaos and lawlessness in his country and elsewhere..."

This edict of excommunication issued on Ghaddafi and widely propagated by Islamic organs of the Saudi government may have been typed out in the chambers of the Grand Council of the Ulema in Riyadh, but it was conceived and written in Reagan's White House! It is almost exactly what the Americans have been saying about Ghaddafi except for the Islamic disguise.

It is in the context of this reality of Saudi Arabia's present regime's role in Africa and the world that one has to place and understand the activities of organisations closely connected with the Saudi-funded Muslim bodies like the Jama'atu Nasirul Islam, the Izala movement, and the Muslim Students Society, whose inspirer and guide is Alhaji Abubakar Gummi.

It is also in this context that one has to place the role that Alhaji Abubakar Gummi is playing in urging Muslims to vote for the N.P.N. and particularly for President Shagari in the 1979 general elections during his radio sermon during the Ramadan *tafsir* of that year.

It is also in this context that one has to understand why somebody like Alhaji Haruna Danja, a large scale landlord, owning hundreds of houses in Zaria and elsewhere; large scale transporter and well-known hoarder of foodstuffs, vehicles and other commodities, is a leading member of the Izala movement inspired and guided by Alhaji Abubakar Gummi The findings of the Shehu Muhammed Judicial Commission of Inquiry of January-May 1976 that this Alhaji Haruna Danja was involved in fraudulent transactions and recycling of large amounts of fertiliser bought for farmers in Kaduna State, cannot be separated from his role in this movement just as it cannot be separated from his role as an N.P.N. member of Kaduna State House of Assembly returned 'unopposed'. It is from such particular examples that the political economy of the manipulation of religion in Nigeria can be constructed stretching from fertiliser distribution depots in Danja to the Chambers of the Grand Council of the Ulema in Riyadh right up to the Pentagon and the White House in Washington and down to Wall Street.

The Israeli Connection

In order to understand the international context of the manipulation of religion in Nigeria today it is necessary to also look at the Israeli factor. This exclusive focus on Saudi Arabia and Israel is not intended to divert attention from the very powerful and permanent role of the Vatican, which as the collapse of the Bank Ambrosiano in Italy recently has illustrated, is involved in direct funding of political parties even outside Italy to sustain regimes subservient to Western imperialism. This is not also to divert attention from the numerous protestant and extra-protestant Christian revivalist organizations funded from America and Europe for all sorts of purposes hostile to the unity of the peoples of Nigeria.

Saudi Arabia and Israel are convenient because of their connections with two of the major political parties of Nigeria, namely the National Party of Nigeria and the Unity Party of Nigeria. Some of the N.P.N.'s connections with Saudi Arabia have already been touched upon. As for the U.P.N., its connection with Israel is through its leader. Chief Obafemi Awolowo, whose annual Christian pilgrimage to Jerusalem even when Israeli troops are massacring Muslim and Christian Lebanese and Palestinians, is an important example of the way religion is manipulated in Nigeria today.

Some Christians in Nigeria have been made to associate with Zionist Israel, because of its association with names that feature in the Bible. The reduction of most Arab anti-Zionism into a religious crusade also promotes this. But increasingly this view is beginning to be questioned, as recent articles in *The Satellite* newspaper of Enugu show, by questioning who exactly is-this 'God of Israel' that sanctioned such inhuman atrocities in Lebanon.

Chief Awolowo's interests include maintaining lucrative business connections with Israeli and other Zionist companies and banks, which like Sole! Boneh enjoy the N.P.N. Federal Government's large-scale patronage, and bring together as their shareholders and directors N.P.N. stalwarts like Chief Akin Deko and the new U.P.N. Deputy-Governor of Oyo State, Chief Akande. But Chief Awolowo's service for Israel and Zionism, cannot be justified, rationally, by any public political principles his party claims to stand for. It includes covering-up Israel's consistent record of backing and arming vicious fascist dictators all over the world. It is an example of the manipulation of religion in Nigeria today.[7]

Conclusion

A systematic study of all the forces involved in this social and political .phenomenon is needed, beyond the evasions and deceptions of the Federal Government. The opaque label of 'religious fanatics' has been, and can easily be, used to cover systematically organised terrorist gangs and death squads to serve forces opposed to the unity progress, and total liberation of the people of this country, The label therefore has to be exposed and the forces involved brought out into the daylight, for the people to see them and decide how best they can, themselves, forge their unity, defend and promote their democratic and civic rights.

Notes

1. See Chapters I and II in this book for some earlier attempts at exposing the real nature of this campaign of the manipulation of religion.

2. See Chapter I of this book.

3. Subsequently both Alhaji Umaru Dikko and Alhaji Turi Muhammadu contested elections to the Senate in 1979 and in 1983 respectively, both on the platform of the National Party of Nigeria (N.P.N.), and were defeated. Their posturing over religion did not assure them the victories in the constituencies with predominantly Muslim populations, which they had expected. Umaru Dikko lost to Alhaji Ibrahim Barau of the People's Redemption Party, who was subsequently jailed on a trumped-up charge of evading custom duties. Since this essay was published in 1982, Umaru Dikko's role in the wrecking of the Nigerian economy in 1979-83, siphoning billions of naira abroad in collaboration with multinational banks and companies, is now too well known to need recounting here. His role illustrates vividly and practically what is being explained in this book, as the real basis of the manipulation of religion in contemporary Nigeria. As for Turi Muhammadu, he went on to a defeat in the 1983 Senatorial elections in the Bida constituency, with a

predominantly Muslim population, by a candidate of the Nigerian Peoples Party (N.P.P.) Dr. Jeremiah Gana, who is a Christian from the same area.

4. This campaign in which the Saudi regime and its agencies like the Muslim World League, also known as 'The Rabitah', took an active part, culminated in the savage American bombings of Libyan cities and ports on Tuesday, 15th April, 1986. The public outrage expressed from all corners of Nigeria at this American aggression showed that the campaign to ostracise Gaddafi as an atheist, conducted by the Saudis and their local agents had failed; so also was the campaign by the Zionists and the American evangelicals against Gaddafi shown to have had only a limited impact. For the campaign to get Nigeria to go to war with Libya in 1980-81, see chapter IV of this book.

5. It is the Nigerian Security Organisation (N.S.O) which mentioned these connections in a report submitted to the Kano Disturbances Tribunal of Inquiry. See *This Week*, vol.4, no.1, 30th March, 1987, p. 22.

6. Throughout all the virulence between the Unity Party of Nigeria (U.P.N.) led by Chief Awolowo and the N.P.N. of Alhaji Shehu Shagari in 1979-83, and the anti-Awolowo campaigns by the Federal Government Kaduna-based media organs accusing him of being pro-Zionist and anti-Islamic, Sole! Boneh the largest Israeli company in Nigeria, contrived to win lucrative contracts from the Federal Government of Shehu Shagari. By December 1983, these had amounted to over ₦200 million.

7. FOR another example of the role of Chief Awolowo and the U.P.N. leadership in the manipulation of religion in Nigeria, see the full text; of the accord reached between the U.P.N. and the Committee of Concerned Citizens. (Appendix B of this book.)

8. The persistence with which imperialism and its agents seek to wreck the unity of Nigeria because of its significance, and potential, for the unity and total liberation of Africa, was eloquently recognised by the late Samora Machel, from as far away as Mozambique. Samora said:

> "In conferring this honour on us, in receiving us in your midst, the teaching staff and students of the Ahmadu Bello University are welcoming the fighting people of Mozambique, a people who, led by FRELIMO, defeated Portuguese colonialism. You are recognising and identifying with the determination of a people who, yesterday oppressed, are now launching an assault on the last bastion of colonial capitalist and racist oppression on our continent. *In the same way, the Mozambican people identify with and recognise the efforts and enthusiasm of the great working people of Nigeria and with their incessant struggle against imperialist designs to divide and weaken them.*" (Speech of acceptance of the degree of Doctor of Laws of Ahmadu Bello University, by Comrade Samora Machel, President of FRELIMO and of the Peoples Republic of Mozambique, A.B.U., Zaria, Saturday, 10th December, 1977.) For full text see *The Analyst*, vol.1, no.4, November 1986.

VII. POLITICAL ECONOMY AND POLITICAL COMMUNITY: THE LESSONS OF THE NINETEENTH CENTURY*

The national question, which is the subject of this seminar, is basically about the form, nature, relationships and motion of political communities. This particular formulation, of course, gives prominence to one type of political community, the nation, which has come to have great significance in world history, for over half a millennium. But to properly comprehend the national question, it has to be seen to be more than about nations and nationalities, but about all forms of political communities, even if in recent world history the nation has been the dominant form.

The Question of Survival

For the people of Africa, the national question is now closely connected with the question of their survival. Their experience over the last quarter of a century has demonstrated that unless this question is faced squarely and new and higher forms of national, and continental, integration are created and forged, at the ecological, economic, social, cultural and political levels, a large proportion of the people of this continent may perish before the end of this century. Moreover, most of those that manage to survive the famines, fratricidal civil wars, chronic undernourishment, chronic

---

* Paper presented at the National Seminar on the National Question, Abuja, 4th-9th August, 1986, as 'Political Economy and Political Community: The Significance of the Nineteenth Century'.

diseases, rural destitution and urban decay, may suffer from physical and mental degeneration in one form or another.

There is nothing sensational or alarmist about this. It is the hard reality of the conditions of life of the people of Africa today, and the immediate threats that face them. It is therefore from these conditions and prospects that all genuine considerations regarding their past, present and future have to take off.

For example, nothing can cover up the fact that in major fratricidal civil wars of Africa, in the 1960's, in , Sudan, Nigeria, Rwanda and Burundi, several millions were killed. The major fratricidal civil wars of Africa of the 1970's and 1980's in Chad, Uganda, Ethiopia, Somalia, and the Sudan are even more intensely devastating of human life and livelihood.

The Ugandan leader, Yoweri Museveni, told the last summit of the Organisation of African Unity at Addis Ababa that 750,000 people were slaughtered in that country under the three regimes of Amin, Obote and the Okellos, which ruled that country. In a small area of Uganda known as the Luwero Triangle, over 100,000 were slaughtered in 1980-86 alone.

The fratricidal civil war in the Sudan and the wars of secession in the Eritrean and Tigrean regions of Ethiopia continue to take a heavy toll of human life.

Millions of Africans within and outside the countries suffering from the fratricidal wars have died as a result of the desertification, droughts, and famines of the early 1970's and 1980's. Many more millions were rendered homeless, landless and destitute in the rural and urban areas all over Africa.

The estimates of those who died in the 1972-74 droughts and the 1982-84 drought seem to be understating the scale of the devastation of human life and the gravity of the threat to human existence that these man-made disasters have caused.

All these devastations of human life and livelihood on our continent are produced largely by the low level of national integration within the nation-states, and between them, and the particular nature of this low level of integration. This is of course more obvious in the case of the civil wars where differences of nationality, ethnicity, and religion are used to create the divisions. But even with the devastations caused by famines and economic crises, a major condition is the level and form of national integration of the productive forces, the most important of which is, of course human mental and manual labour.[1]

The people of Nigeria have not only been devastated by these civil wars, famines, unemployment, urban decay and rural destitution, but are still being devastated and are threatened with further devastations. For besides the established political forces which have successfully maintained a low level of national integration in the country, a virulent form of sectionalist and secessionist political campaign has developed over the last decade. Political groupings and tendencies of apparently divergent and even opposing, religious and ethnic colouring have been pushing persistently for the dismemberment of the country along religious and ethnic-lines, a process which will obviously involve a bloody and protracted civil war. They are doing this under the cover of the campaign for the Shari'a and the creation of an Islamic state in Nigeria, on the one hand, and on the other, the need for a confederation ostensibly in order to 'allow every ethnic and religious group to develop at its own pace, along its own lines and according to its own aptitude'. ,

The most easily identifiable political groupings involved in this persistent and increasingly well-orchestrated campaign are the upper class commission agents, brokers, and their intellectuals, of three ostensibly opposed tendencies made up mainly of the protagonists of the 'Republic of Oduduwa', the Biafran rump, and the Committee of Concerned Citizens of the Kaduna Mafia, and the Shari'a lobby they control.[2]

All these three tendencies generally seem to have in common powerful external patronage from America either directly, or .through Israel, Saudi Arabia and the Gulf Sheikdoms, and other countries.

The effective and systematic way the Constituent Assembly was polarised, ostensibly over Shari'a, in 1978 and had its sittings end abruptly, after generating tension all over the country; the current controversy over Nigeria's connection with the Organization of the Islamic Conference; and the more recent generation of rancour and bitterness over the sites of places of worship in the University of Ibadan campus, illustrate very clearly that the people of Nigeria are faced with a well-orchestrated threat, which makes the national question in this country today, a matter of immediate significance for its continued survival as a single entity. And the experiences of the last quarter of a century in this country, and in the rest of the continent, this threat of disintegration involves the threat of physical devastation of the lives and livelihood of tens of millions of its people.

This paper is an attempt at contributing to an understanding of this question by attempting a preliminary exploration of the nineteenth century transformations of the political communities from which the country emerged in the twentieth century. The nineteenth century is important because so much in Nigerian society and politics which is passed off as 'natural', 'traditional', 'cultural' and 'indigenous' is drawn from the historical experiences during that century. It is hoped that this preliminary exploration will enable us to begin to grasp the substance of the historical processes that shape and determine the emergence and notion of this country as a political community.

Historicity

Although there is now available a major study of the national question in Nigeria which has successfully taken it beyond the racist stereotypes of colonial anthropology and historiography, and the mythical dualities of tradition and modernity, this study. *Ethnic Politics in Nigeria,* by Okwudiba Nnoli,[3] denies the relevance of the historical process before colonialism in comprehending the question Nigeria.

The picture he paints of the pre-colonial societies is both romantic, uniform and static. Regarding the economy of the pre-colonial societies as it relates to ethnicity, Nnoli says:

"Colonialism ushered in a period of significant scarcity through the importation of the capitalist mode
of production from outside. Prior to it various pre-
capitalist modes of production prevailed each with
its characteristic social formation. However, they
shared certain features in common including a low
level of production, underdeveloped productive
forces, and a meagre surplus from production...
Each member of the society was gainfully

employed in accordance with the prevailing norms and the local physical and biological environments. More importantly relative deprivation was not *a* component of the perceptual map of the population. Within the norms of society, each individual accepted his station in life and therefore, his share of the surplus from production. There was no discrepancy between the expected and the actual patterns of benefits. Above all there was no divergence between the pattern of consumption and the needs of the vast majority of the population. The importation of the capitalist mode of production through colonialism disrupted this organic link between the pattern of the use of resources, and the needs and consumption habits of the population, It thereby created scarcity at both objective and subjective levels."[4]

And:

"Having been uprooted from the pre-colonial setting which had valid meaning for him, in which history had effectively and organically related him to his local environment and culture had produced salutary patterns of .interactions with others, the African migrant found the door to the coloniser's glorified world securely barred to him. The resultant anomie and alienation affected his socio-economic and political activities. Even in interactions with his fellow Africans he experienced tensions, anxiety, and insecurity. Disoriented, subjugated and humiliated by the coloniser he directed his aggressive impulses against other colonised 'natives' with whom he competed on the basis of equality. Ethnic group membership was useful for this competition".[5]

In an even more explicit fashion Nnoli denies the relevance of the pre-colonial historical process to the nature of ethnicity in Nigeria. He says that:

"In Nigeria the colonial urban setting constitutes the cradle of contemporary ethnicity. As will become evident later it was there that what we refer to today as ethnic groups first acquired a common consciousness. In other words contemporary Nigerian ethnicity is not the result of some barbarous mystique peculiar to the African. Nor is it basically the consequence of the pre-colonial patterns of conflict among the various pre-colonial.' polities. In fact in the various Nigerian languages there is no equivalent concept for tribalism".[6]

This romantic, and essentially static, view of pre-colonial Nigerian society is ahistorical. But significantly when it comes to the examination of the national question even one of the leading Nigerian historians, Ade Ajayi, accedes to an ahistorical view.

In a recent lecture, Ajayi recognised that in the past there were historical movements creating village communities from clans, ethnic groups from villages, into kingdoms, into empires and into multinational states.[7] He also recognised that the process of integration was a historical process. He gives a lot of importance to the role of a common language which he treats almost as the same as a common culture, in this process of integration.[8]

But when it comes down to the actual process of the formation of the peoples of Nigeria he banishes it to an obscure past, saying that:

"The origin of most of the component peoples and cultures of Nigeria lie in the obscure past and it is not possible at this stage to demonstrate or even illustrate how the different polities emerged." [9]

From this 'obscure past' Professor Ajayi conceives of what he calls 'traditional cultures and institutions' which he says still enjoy the loyalties of our people giving them their sense of identity.[10] These 'traditional cultures' he characterises as follows:

"Most traditional cultures in Nigeria stressed the virtues of social and political integration. This was done in various ways: through proverbs and political precepts; through the world view implicit in religious doctrines emphasising the unbroken chain between the ancestors; above all through the body of oral traditions which represent the group memory and the collective view of the shared past. These traditions generally seemed to have rated continuity and stability above innovation and change."[11]

Thus while Professor Ajayi recognises integration as a historical process and gives a lot of importance to language, culture and ecology in the process, when it comes down to the actual process of the formation of the peoples of Nigeria and their contemporary cultures and identities he resorts to a rather ahistorical view even if less romantic than the one taken by Nnoli. .Obaro Ikime in a recent lecture seems to

111

have brought out more clearly the historicity, of the process of the creation of the nationalities of Nigeria. He says that:

"One, the nationalities which today constitute the Nigerian nation did not exist as functional socio-political entities until this century. Two, that it was the sub-groups within these nationalities that constituted meaningful socio-political entities. Three, that even the sub-groups were the product of deliberate acts of statesmanship; the results of negotiated unions and the amalgamation now clothed in legends of common origin."[12]

And that:

"In the heat of modern politics and in the struggle for a fair share of the nation's resources, the leaders of the various ethnic and other groups which constitute Nigeria naturally take the existence of these groups for granted. It is almost as if these groups, these people of Nigeria, have always been identified as Hausa, Fulani, Yoruba, Efik, Ijaw, Tiv, Idoma, Ebira, Igala, Itsekiri, Jukun, Bini, Ishan, Isoko, Urhobo, etc. Yet we know, don't we, that these did not begin to identify themselves in these terms until the emergence of the colonial state of Nigeria. Indeed it would be right to argue that it was the European visitors, traders and writers who first began to refer to whole conglomerates in terms of the language they speak. When such foreigners referred to the Igbo they meant those who speak that language, not a single politically coherent group. Our ethnic groups, our nationalities, are thus essentially linguistic and cultural groups that have been increasingly forced by circumstances of history to act politically in defence of their interests vis-a-vis the interests of competing groups in what we know as Nigeria. This is clearly a 20th century development".[13]

Ikime seems to bring history back into the process of the formation of the nationalities of Nigeria. But in fact the distinction he forces between what he calls "the essentially linguistic and cultural groups" of pre-colonial Nigeria and the ethnic groups and nationalities produced under colonialism, actually throws history out of the window, at least as far as the formation of Nigerian nationalities in the period before colonialism is concerned.

In fact when later in the lecture he comes down to dealing with aspects of Nigerian history before colonialism, he implicitly recognises that the ethnic groups and nationalities of contemporary Nigeria were not just products of defensive reactions since the imposition of the colonial state, by "essential linguistic and cultural groups". This recognition comes out in his references to the Sokoto Jihad and the Hausa-Fulani nationality.[14]

The denial of the relevance of the historical process before colonial domination to the national question in Nigeria by Nnoli; and the ambivalence and ambiguities on the part of Ajayi and Ikime, when it comes down to the actual process of the formation of the nationalities of contemporary Nigeria, seem to indicate that the problem is more than that of ahistoricity. It seems that the problem is that what constitutes the substance of the process of the formation of all political communities, including nations and nationalities, is not clearly grasped by these writers, because they do not perceive political identity, language and culture in the context of the political economy of political communities.

The Basic Relations

A political community whether it is a clan, a village, a village-group, a city, a kingdom, a republic, a nation-state, a caliphate, an alafinate, or empire, is not just made up of people bound together at the level of language, culture, identity and territory. The human beings who constitute all political communities – and without human beings there are no political communities of any type – are themselves products of certain basic, and regular, relationships which constitute the foundation of all societies, at all times.

The two basic elements of these relations are those for the reproduction of human beings, and secondly, those for the production of the means for the sustenance of human beings.

The reproduction of human beings is an activity which goes beyond the acts of conception and procreation. These acts alone produce only the human biological specie. The human being, who is a social being, having the capacity for manual and mental activity, including language, is produced, beyond conception and procreation, by feeding, nurturing, socialisation, acculturation, training, education and orientation.

The production of the means for the sustenance of life, and of the capacity and means of producing these means, are closely integrated with the activity of reproducing human beings, because human mental and manual labour is the motor and engine of all these.

Human beings speaking the Ibo, Yoruba, Hausa or Isoko languages do not drop from the sky, or come out of holes in the ground. They are reproduced by the productive activity of other human beings. These involve procreation, nurturing, feeding, training, education, and orientation, and the production of food and tools.

Human beings who believe in Sango, Orisa, Ubangiji, Chukwu, or Allah and worship the deity in various places and in various ways, do not fall from trees or are carried around by the wind. They are reproduced by the manual and mental labour of other human beings in regular relation with one another and with natural objects.

Neither do human beings obtain their political identities in any other place, or in any other way outside the process of their own reproduction, the production of the means for sustaining human life, and the reproduction of others. All these are carried on in particular territorial locations, adapting and utilising the natural environment they find.

And, since this activity of reproducing human beings and their means of sustenance is the foundation of human existence, creating language, culture, political identity and giving relevance to territory, it is the relations that human beings enter into in the course of these activities, which are necessary and imperative for human survival, that we must examine in order to understand the substance of political communities of whatever type.

These relations are called social relations of production, and vary a great deal in accordance with the level of the productive forces in the society, its division of labour, the way the product of this labour (including the labour used in producing human beings) is shared out and utilised.

A look at these relations and the way they were changing in the nineteenth century may take us to the substance of the historical movement of the political

115

communities which came to form Nigeria in the 20th century. Before doing that, however, let us look at the form of these political communities and the way these forms were changing in the nineteenth century.

The Forms of the Transformation

The nineteenth century was a period of major changes in the nature and scope of the polities of Nigeria and many other parts of the African continent, from the Drakensberg Mountains in the far south to the Nile Delta on the Mediterranean; from the Senegal Valley to the Ethiopian Highlands. These changes and their importance has been recognised in many studies of African history and society, but their form, nature and substance has not been tackled on a sufficiently comprehensive basis to establish a general picture over most of the continent. The rough outline sketched out here is very much a preliminary exploration using some of the historical evidence available on Nigeria. It is hoped that this will stimulate more serious exercises in order to grasp the motion of our societies and history at a level at which deeper insights into current conditions and directions can be attained, and used for effective political activity to ensure the survival and progress of all our people. In Nigeria in the nineteenth century, the changes that occurred took diverse forms. The dominant pattern which this writer can see is that of the ossification, withering, paralysis, collapse and overthrow of the established governments and political communities, and the attempts to replace them with more powerful governments and larger and more coherent political communities, with a much more heterogeneous national composition and a more universalistic basis.

The most closely studied aspect of this process was the collapse and overthrow of the governments and polities of the *sarakuna* of the *kasashe* of Hausaland, the *mais* of the Bornoan Caliphate, the Etsus of Nupe, the Alafins of Oyo, in the first half of the 19th century; and the establishment of the Sokoto Caliphate, the Sultanate of Borno under the Kanemi Sheikhs, and the city states of Ibadan and Abeokuta.

Alongside these better-known changes were the lesser-known collapse of the Oluship of Warri; the withering of the Obaship of Benin; the ossification of the Attahship of Igala; the decline in the hegemony of the Aro and other merchant oligarchies of south-eastern Nigeria; and the emergence along the coast from Lagos to Calabar, of new merchants of slave and commoner origin challenging the old oligarchies, and the Benin aristocracy, and the various Igbo communal gerontocracies.[15] In the Middle Benue Basin and in the Niger-Benue Confluence Area, new political authorities, concentrating in themselves new wealth, political and military power, were emerging in the form of the *toragbande* (drum chiefs) among the Tiv, and the *ako* (strongman) among the Igbirra Tao.[16]

These transformations of the 19th century were on a scale and with a tempo which was quite unprecedented in Nigerian history, particularly at the demographic, social and political levels.

A city-state like Ibadan would rise from a village in 1827 to a city of about 60,000 people in 1852, and about 150,000 by 1890, with walls of about 28.8 kilometres in circumference, made up of people drawn from almost all the nationalities and sub-nationalities of the Yoruba, and from the Nupe, Hausa and others.[17] Moreover, it was ruled, not by a monarch claiming autochtonous legitimacy and hereditary feudal authority, but by self-made warriors and merchants of diverse origin.[18]

The city of Bida grew from a small Nupe village in the 1850's, into the capital of one of the most powerful, and richest, emirates of the Sokoto Caliphate, with a population of about 110,000 in 1868.[19] Bida was made up of, and surrounded by, wards, guilds, hamlets; agricultural estates filled with artisans, peasants, serfs and slaves of very diverse origins drawn from all the nationalities of the neighbouring areas.[20]

The capital city of the Sokoto Caliphate itself, Birnin, Sokoto, and the rest of the metropolis, saw similarly rapid expansion from a small hamlet in 1809 to a city of over 100,000 by the end of the century, surrounded by densely peopled rural areas and large cities like Birnin Kebbi, Gusau, Isa and Kaura Namoda, all of great heterogeneous composition, with nationalities drawn from all over western Africa and the Sahara.[21]

This transformation went from Kukuwa, to Yola, to Muri, to Norm, down to Abeokuta, Aboh, Osomari, and to Opobo.

These new urban centres and the expanding old ones like Birnin Kano, Birnin Zaria, Old Calabar and Lagos, together with the rural areas around them, constituted the component units of the new political communities, in their heterogeneity and in the more universalistic basis of their incorporation.

This basis is often recognised in its application to the Sokoto Caliphate and Borno. The significance of Islam in providing the ideological basis for the new political communities made up of people of more heterogeneous origin than the old polities could incorporate, is widely recognised.

This is also, sometimes, acknowledged in the case of Ibadan, where a new political ideology, whose articulation has not been properly studied, clearly involved a rejection of the restrictive claims of feudal autochtony in favour of a more universalistic basis of incorporating people of diverse origins, giving a lot of importance to military and mercantile capabilities.[22]

However, what is not so often recognised is that what happened in the Sokoto Caliphate, Borno and Ibadan also took place, even if less well-studied, in the village-groups and city-states of the Igbo, Efik, Ibibio, Ijaw and other peoples of South-eastern Nigeria. In these areas merchant oligarchies became very powerful in several ways; one of the most obvious being through the economic and political power that the titled associations, secret societies, and cults like theEkpe, the Okonko and Ndi Nze came to exercise.[23] These clearly began to overshadow and subordinate, or subvert, the autochtonous gerontocracies and older oligarchies in these polities. The kinship terminology that prevailed in the political discourse in these societies where the communal mode of production remained politically significant, has tended to obscure this trend in these societies in the 19th century.[24]

This process of the emergence of new classes and strata concentrating in themselves wealth, military and political power, over and above the elders and priests, also occurred in the Middle Benue Basin and the Niger Benue Confluence Area. Among the Tiv, for *agbandes* like Chia Chire (c.1880-85) of the Mbagan, Aba Kum of the Kpav, Abuul Benga of the

Mbagwa, and Dajo of the Ikum, concentrated wealth and power in their hands; and Abuul Benga even had a private army, while others hired Hausa-Jukun mercenaries under Dankaro and such adventurers from the emirates.[25]

Among the Igbirra Tao, the Ajinomoh War of the 1860's produced powerful warrior-merchants (ako) like the Attah Omadibi Abanika of Igbirra-lgala parentage.[26]

But what is important for our purpose of examining the relationship between political economy and political community is that the levels of cohesion and integration that the new political communities seemed to set out to attain, and which the threat of European imperialist invasion called for as an elementary requirement for defence, were never attained.[27] While in some places the ideal remained and became the basis of political contestation and struggle, the fact was that generally all over Nigeria the historical momentum of this process of transformation was dissipated before the colonial invasion and conquest late in the 19th and in the early 20th century.

The Sokoto Caliphate came to be torn by a series of intense and violent civil wars in its richest and most powerful emirates, where the process of incorporating people of diverse origin into the new political communities seemed to have advanced rapidly. These took place in Bauchi Emirate in 1881; in Bida Emirate in 1881-82; in Kano Emirate in 1893-95; and in a chronic fashion in Muri in the 1890's.[28]

Alongside these civil wars, serious radical challenges to the Caliphate and the emirate ruling class emerged from sections of the intelligentsia, peasants, slaves, traders, herdsmen and artisans, discontented with the closed, affluent aristocracies, whose extortions and illegalities increased as

120

their vision of an Islamic political community to incorporate all the people of the *bilad al-Sudan* disappeared. This radical challenge took its most politically concrete form in the principality of Balda, established near the Mandara Mountains by a Sokoto prince, Hayatu b. Said, in the late 1880's; and in the Imamate of Burmi carved out of Gombe Emirate by the rebellion fed by Mallam Jibrilla in 1887.[29] These two small polities, in spite of their small size, posed a serious ideological, political and military challenge to the narrow and oppressive Caliphate and emirate aristocracies, partly because of their egalitarian and much more cohesive mode of incorporation.[30] The fact that the most powerful resistance put up against the British invasion of the Caliphate was by the citizens of the new Imamate of Burmi behind the Caliph Attahirun Ahmadu, in contrast with the paralysis and supine submission of most the Caliphate's aristocracy, demonstrates how significant these new communities were, notwithstanding Hayatu's misadventure with Rabih.

The attempt in Borno by the Shehu Muhammad Al-Kanemi to counter the Sokoto Jihad and rejuvenate Borno on a more cohesive and effective Islamic basis had clearly not advanced far by the 1880's. Deep discontent, intensified by exacting taxation and chronic divisions among the ruling class, made it easy for Rabih to conquer a Sheikhdom clearly lacking in cohesion.

The thrust of Ibadan to constitute itself as the core of a new polity incorporating most of the Yoruba nationalities had, by 1886, failed, mired in the protracted Kiriji War of 1878-86.[32]

In south-eastern Nigeria the merchant oligarchies, whether of the older or of the newer variety, had come under

British hegemony and attempts to widen the scope of their ruling classes, even as middlemen of the palm oil trade, were curbed by the British. And Benin continued in its "decline and disintegration from within".[33]

The question that immediately arises is why did the process of transformation of political communities all over what came to be Nigeria take place when it did? And, secondly, why did it suffer the limitations it did? One obvious explanation is the dynamics of European imperialism, which, basically independent of what was taking place in Nigeria, was from the 1870's engaged in subjugating Africa under direct colonial domination. But even with this explanation the question arises as to why this very act of invasion and conquest did not provide a stimulus to generate movements of resistance which would provide a new framework for forging ahead with more cohesive political communities. Why, for example, did the aristocracy of the Sokoto Caliphate and the merchants and warriors of Ibadan submit to the British so supinely compared to others with far fewer resources, human and material, and in more limited and worse terrain? More specifically, what was it that enabled the successors of Chaka to defeat a powerful British army with their *impis* in 1879, and those of Shehu Usman Dan Fodio to so easily surrender in 1903? This hard and concrete historical reality cannot be evaded in the examination of the form and nature of the political community of Nigeria in the nineteenth century.

The Substance of the Transformation

It was from this historical process, and the way it developed under colonial conquest and domination, that the nationalities of contemporary Nigeria emerged. Any serious consideration of the national question in Nigeria has to comprehend its form, substance and direction.

The Igbo, Efik, Hausa, Fulbe, Hausa-Fulani, Nupe, Yoruba, Tiv and other nationalities of contemporary Nigeria were not just formed in the colonial urban centres in the course of some defensive struggle for schools, jobs, markets, land and credit. Neither do their identities have their roots there.

At the same time it is obvious that the formation of these nationalities is not something that occurred in some obscure past through the integrative force of some traditional cultures.

To comprehend the nature and relationships of the nationalities of Nigeria we have to go beyond all these into the basic relations at the foundation of the societies of Nigeria. These relations have not been static, uniform or monolithic. They are organised in complex patterns of congruence and contradictions. In spite of the limited historical evidence regarding the reproductive and the pro-ductive activity of man in Nigerian societies, it is possible, at least for the nineteenth century, to identify two distinct socio-economic systems prevailing over most of Nigeria. A socio-economic system made up of a distinct complex of relations of production and productive forces is what is known as a mode of production. And it is to the examination of these that we must turn if we want to grasp the substance of the historical process of the transformation of the political communities in Nigeria. This process cannot be explained in terms of traditional cultures or pre-colonial statesmanship, or the competition, anomie and exploitation of colonialism.

Over a large part of the Nigerian area during the nineteenth century, it is possible to identify a distinct socio-economic system underlying many of the societies and polities. This socio-economic system or mode of production is basically characterised by common ownership of the means of production, collective labour and collective appropriation of the products of labour, with families, lineages, clans and other kinship units constituting the basic cells of the organisation of social production. This mode of production is known as the communal mode of production and exists with a great deal of variations.

In Nigeria during the nineteenth century, we also find societies and polities another mode of prod-different from the one organised around families and clans. This other one is the feudal mode of production. This mode of production is basically characterised by the control and appropriation of the labour, and products of labour, of *subjects* by their *lords*. This ownership control and appropriation of the labour of the subject bythe lord is centered primarily on land, and takes a complex variety of forms of subordination, servility, individuation, and institutionalisation, stretching from the almost private feudal manors of early English feudalism, to the tributary and bureaucratic form it takes in China, Egypt and the states of Hausaland.

These two modes of production, the communal and the feudal, seem to be the most prevalent in the Nigerian area in the 19th century. But there was incorporated within them, in varied ways, slavery, not as a distinct mode of production, but as an important element in the range of servile status found in both the feudal systems and the communal ones. Merchant capital whose significance is of some antiquity in this area and has an important role within both modes of production, one of the most important of which is the expansion of the market for staples and slaves, or labour and for export, across the Atlantic or the Sahara.

It would appear that by the nineteenth century the political communities of Nigeria, with both feudal and communal foundations, were held together by social, political, cultural and legal relations which were increasingly constraining the production and exchange of goods and services, and even the reproduction of human labour. This constraint was in the form of taboos, laws, taxes, levies, fees, customs, monopolies, and caused by the entrenched sectionalisation necessary to sustain feudal and communal autochtony. The penetration of these polities by merchant capital which had accelerated in the fifteenth and sixteenth centuries, with the consolidation of the major feudal states, from Borno to Benin, had expanded the market and promoted domestic and export slavery, peonage, and other client and servile relationships. This process had also been accompanied by and promoted migrations of artisans, traders, herdsmen, fishermen, and other productive strata. All this was straining the political basis of feudal and communal autochtony, and the privileges of their gerontocracies, aristocracies and guilds.

When the feudal states conquered new subjects, they exacted tributes from them, but their systems prevented the incorporation of even the upper strata of these conquered peoples as citizens of their polity. The process of socialisation, acculturation, education and training essential for this incorporation was blocked and hindered by the exclusive privileges, rituals, customs, taboos and whole social, political, ideological and cultural superstructure of polities, whose basis of cohesion, and whose rulers' legitimacy, is rooted in some form of communal or feudal autochtony.

The strains and stresses produced by this contradiction, between the way the productive forces of the society and its division of labour was developing, and the dominant political, legal, religious and cultural order, was obviously much sharper in the more centralised feudal systems than in the communal ones.

Muslim merchants or artisans among the Yagba, Akoko or Ijumu could be made to constitute a 'lineage' and somehow-adapted in a communal, non-hierarchical system. But Muslim merchants and artisans in Oyo-lle or Igboho raise issues and problems which could be politically explosive, for the political, legal and cultural order of the Alafinate, as was demonstrated in the Afonja revolt and the jihad.

The new states that were emerging out of the upheavals of the first half of the nineteenth century, particularly those of the Sokoto Caliphate and the city-states of Ibadan, could not significantly break the fetters imposed on the productive forces by feudal autochtony because their ruling classes came to be tied up with the activities of merchants, who promoted the slave trade and the export-orientation towards North Africa and the Atlantic, whether involving slaves or other commodities. Merchant capital has always gained and flourished on the basis of monopolies, exclusive privileges, guilds, and all the taboo, ritual and secrecy which separates one market from another effectively enough to maximise the merchant's profit. When these merchants were also closely involved in slave trading, whether for domestic or export purposes, their role and that of the aristocracy or warrior oligarchies tied up with this, will strongly favour the preservation of these restrictions and constraints on the productive forces, particularly the movement of human, agricultural, artisan, and other forms of labour.

The ideal of the Sokoto Jihad was to build a political community of Muslim citizens for the *bilad af-Sudan* who would be integrated into a cohesive *umma*, over and above all other differences. But the feudal mode of production of the caliphate, and the powerful role of merchant capital in political and military activities, particularly in the area of revenue, entrenched slavery, tributes, corvee, privileges, and restrictive monopolies.

Muslim law and precedent allows for slavery and slave trade. But the ideal since the days of Medina was to free all slaves and make them full Muslim citizens. Conversion and citizenship was also the ideal for the non-Muslim peoples, particularly those who are neither Jews nor Christians. These *dhimmi* were, particularly, to be converted to Islam and made full citizens of the Muslim polity.

The feudal mode of production of the Sokoto Caliphate and the way the aristocracy that emerged from its rulers was closely tied up with merchants, local and foreign, in tribute and tax matters, warfare, banking and finance and external trade, made the serious pursuit of these ideals impossible. The *dhimmi* were preserved for enslavement. And the many among them who became Muslims after their enslavement, or their children and grandchildren, were still kept as slaves or under some form of serfdom or servile status.

The legitimacy for collecting land tax and tribute from Muslim village communities did not exist. But the requirement of this aristocracy – its fiscal, merchant and military strata– ensured that this illegitimacy became a matter of state policy. Perhaps the best example of this whole contradiction was the conflict between Sarkin Gwaram Lawal and the Emir of Bauchi Umaru b. Salmanu, over the attempt to enslave former *dhimmi* who had become Muslims and citizens of the city of Gwaram of Bauchi Emirate. This conflict ended in the sacking of Gwaram and the enslavement of about 9,000 of its citizens.

Gwaram had, by 1900 when it was sacked, developed into one of the richest cities of Bauchi Emirate, founded by migrant Kano *mallamai* in the 19th century. It was sited in a fertile area and attracted migrants from all over the Bauchi region. The trade routes to Muri and Adamawa passed through it. Dyeing, weaving and iron working rapidly developed. The hamlets surrounding it like Kachi-chiya, Nasarawa, and Tudun Wada became centres of agriculture and pastoralism. It was also known as a town of devout Muslim citizens, in many ways a model city for the urbanisation policy of the Sokoto Caliphate. Some the immigrants who made up its very heterogeneous population were from Fali, and were former *dhimmi*. The Chief of Fali told the Emir of Bauchi that some of the slaves he had kept for him to send as tribute to Sokoto were among the Fali *dhimmi* who had migrated to Gwaram.

The Emir of Bauchi, Umar, who had been appointed to heal the bitter wounds of the 1881-82 civil war demanded that these people be given over to him. The Sarkin Gwaram Lawal refused. After several months of confrontation, Gwaram was sacked, the Sarkin Gwaram Lawal was executed by Emir Umar, and about 9,000 of its citizens enslaved. The Caliph at Sokoto was angered, and rejected the slaves sent to him from

128

among the Muslim population of Gwaram. The Bauchi court *ulama* however justified this in their writings on the grounds that the people of Gwaram had revolted and committed apostasy.

Similarly, the activities of the merchants of Ibadan among the Ijesa and Ekiti, over tribute, taxes, tolls and the use. of Ibadan's *ajeles* to get trading monopolies and privileges, made it impossible for the people of these areas to get incorporated into a new polity and a new citizenry above the old divisions.

The significance of all these developments relating to the political economy of the political communities of Nigeria in the nineteenth century is that it brings out the level at which these communities were constituted, and therefore the level at which the nationalities of contemporary Nigeria were formed, go deeper than political institutions, constitutions, etc.

The process of the integration of people into new nationalities and nations is a process which is basically located at the level of change in the social relations of production and the productive forces.

Conclusion

As has been pointed out at the beginning of this paper, there should be no doubt about the fact that for the people of Nigeria, and the rest of Africa, the national question is now a question of survival. Without new and higher forms of national and continental integration, tens of millions of people in this country, and in this continent, are likely to perish, before the end of this century, in fratricidal civil wars and man-made ecological and economic disasters. It is therefore a very serious question.

The lessons of our historical experience in the nineteenth century, as far as the national question is concerned at the general level, is to show that the historical process of creating more cohesive political communities, integrating people of heterogeneous origin, was a manifestation of developments which had their roots at the level of changes in the social relations of production and the productive forces of the societies of Nigeria in that century; and that the serious limitations that this process of creation and integration faced were also rooted at the same level of basic relations and forces.

This shows that we cannot comprehend the nature and direction of political community, whether it is the city state of Old Calabar with its Efik, Ibibio, Igbo and other nationalities; or Borno or the Sokoto Caliphate, with their powerful states and multiple nationalities; or even the sovereign confederation of clans, the *tar*. among the Tiv, with a less heterogeneous national composition; or the Nigerian nation-state, with its multiplicity of nationalities, without going beyond constitutions, charters, laws, political institutions, political behaviour, formulae for sharing appointments, culture, and psychology, into the basic relations which constitute the foundation of these communities.

The seriousness of the national question makes it imperative for us to go into these deeper levels of the basic relations at the foundation of our political communities. Communal and feudal relations of production had in the 19th century blocked the process of the emergence of more cohesive political communities in Nigeria which could have defeated the invasion by British imperialism. This was in spite of the fact that there was a powerful political momentum towards such political communities in the first half of the century in many areas.

When the British conquered Nigeria, with comparatively limited resistance, they found some of the aspects of these communal and feudal relations useful and subordinated them within the colonial capitalist relations of production they established. The vested interests of communal and feudal autochtony now linked with more modern mercantile forces have promoted the segmentation and fragmentation of the productive forces of Nigeria and constitute powerful obstacles to integrated and independent national development. These interests, in the form of emirs, obas, obis, shehus, various types of chieftaincies, titled associations, and cults, opposed the ideological and political integration of the people of Nigeria, across the nationalities, during the struggle for national independence, and they have continued to play the same role in the contemporary struggle for national liberation.

The complete and definitive abolition of these vestiges of feudal and communal autochtony; the thoroughgoing democratisation of all levels of society by popular organisations of peasants, workers, artisans, youth, women, and all those constituting the human core of the productive forces of the country; and the building of an independent socialist economy and society, on this foundation, are three essential requirements for forging Nigeria into a cohesive, and united, multi-national state, which alone can ensure our survival and progress into the next century.

Notes

1. The critical significance of the low-level, and perverse, integration of the productive forces of the Nigerian economy is treated in our book: *The Nigerian Economic Crisis: Causes and Solutions,* by Alkasum Abba, et al). ASUU, Zaria, 1985.

2. For one of the few public evidences of the congruence between the Committee of Concerned Citizens of the Kaduna Mafia and one of the two other tendencies see "Our Pact with Awo: Committee of Concerned Citizens", *Nigerian Tribune,* 6th August, 1983; and the support for 'Confederation' given by Dr. Suleiman Kumo. a member of the Committee, in the *New Nigerian,* 18th June, 1986. The text of that 'Covenant' signed with Chief Awolowo, for the 1983 presidential elections, divided Nigeria into regional and religious blocs, with the Kaduna Mafia representing 'the North' and 'Muslims'. See Appendix B of this book.

3. *Ethnic Politics in Nigeria,* by Okwudiba Nnoli, Fourth Dimension Publishers, Enugu, 1980. In spite of all its limitations this study is a major contribution, which in the decade since it was written has not been surpassed by anything as comprehensive and detailed.

4. Nnoli, p.76.

5. Nnoli, p. 22.

6. Nnoli, p. 35.

7. *The Problems of National Integration in Nigeria: A Historical Perspective,* by J.F.A. Ajayl, 11th Nigerian Institute of Social and Economic Research, Distinguished Lecture, University of Sokoto, Sokoto, 11th December, 1984 (mimeo).

8. Ajayi.

9. Ajayi.

10. Ajayi.

11. Ajayi.

12. *In Search of Nigerians: Changing Patterns of Inter-Group Relations in an Evolving Nation,* by Obaro Ikime, Presidential Inaugural Lecture delivered at the 30th Congress of the Historical Society of Nigeria, Nsukka, 1st May 1985. Historical Society of Nigeria, Ibadan, 1985, p.5.

13. Ikime, pp. 3-4.

14. Ikime, p.6.

15. *Benin and the Europeans: 1485-1897,* by A.F.C. Ryder, Longman, 1977; *Trade without Rulers: Pre-Colonial Economic Development in South-Eastern Nigeria,* by David Northrup, Clarendon, 1978; and *The Nupe Kingdom in the Nineteenth Century: A Political History,* by Michael Mason, PhD; Thesis, University of Birmingham.

16. *A History of Political Change Among the Tiv in the 19th and 20th Centuries,* by Tesem Makar, Ph.D. Thesis, A.B.U* 1975, pages 192-197; and *The Search for Leadership in a Nigerian Community: The Igbirra Tao, 1865-1954,* by Y.A. Ibrahim, M.A. Thesis, A.B.U., 1968, page 81.

17. *The Political Economy of a Pre-Colonial African State: Ibadan, 1830-1900,* by Toyin Falola, University of Ife Press, 1984; and "The Economic Foundations of Ibadan's Power in the Nineteenth Century" by S.A. Akintoye, in *Topics on Nigerian Economic and Social History,* (ed) I.A, Akinjogbin and S.O. Osoba, University of Ife Press, 1980, page 65.

18. Falola, page 45, page 65.

19. Mason, page 435.

20. Mason, pages 428-29; and "Captive and Client Labour and the Economy of Bida Emirate: 1857-1901", M. Mason, *Journal of African History,* Vol. XIV, IMo.3, 1973, page 460.

21. *Studies in the History of the Sokoto Caliphate: The Sokoto Seminar Papers,* (ed) Y.B. Usman, Third Press International, New York, 1979; and A. Mabogunje, *Urbanisation in Nigeria,* University of London Press, London, 1968.

22. *Revolution and Power Politics in Yorubaland 1840-1893: Ibadan and the Rise of the Ekiti Parapo,* by S.A. Akintoye, Longmans, Ibadan, pages 212-14.

23. Northrup, page 111; and "Trade and Trade Routes in 19th Century Nsukka", by A, Afigbo, *Journal of the Historical Society of Nigeria,* Vol. VII, No.1, 1973.

24. A society can produce a particular language of political discourse which can give the impression that certain relations are very important because of the way they feature In the Idiom of that language.

25. Makar, pages 192-97.

26. Ibrahim, pages 81-83.

27. S.C. Ukpabi in his studies of the British invasion and conquest of Nigeria has always emphasized how the lack of political cohesion and military cooperation within and between Nigerian polities made the defeat of these polities easier. Defeat in a war, not just in a battle, which leads a polity to lose its sovereignty and become colonised is a very serious matter. It is significant that those who nowadays advocate that Nigeria should return to political systems like those of the Sokoto Caliphate or Benin, evade the historical importance of the conquest of these polities by the British.

28. Mason; *The Establishment and Development of Emirate Government in Bauchi: 1805-1903*, by A. Y. Abubakar, Ph.D. Thesis, A.B.U., 1974; *The Imposition of British Colonial Domination on the Sokoto Caliphate, Borno and Neighbouring States: 1897-1914*, by M.M. Tukur, Ph.D. Thesis, A.B.U,, 1979; and *The Rise and Fall of the Emirate of Muri (Hammaruwa): C. 1812-1903*, by Mahmoud Harnman, Ph.D. Thesis, A.B,U., 1983.

29. *The Mahdist Tradition in Northern Nigeria, by* Mohammed AI-Hajj, Ph.D. Thesis, A.B.U., 1973, pages 114-141; and "Adamawa and Mahdlsm: The Career of Hayatu Ibn Said in Adamawa", by M.Z. Njeuma, *Journal of African History*, Vol.XII, No.1, 1971, pages 61-7.

30. Njeuma, pages 66-67.

31. "A Preliminary Investigation into the Revenue System of the Borno Government in the 19th Century", by A. K. Benisheikh, *Topics on Nigerian Economic and Social History*,(ed) I. A. Akinjogbin and S.O. Osoba, Ife, 1980.

32. Falola; and Akintoye, *Revolution and Power Politics.*

33. "The   Pre-Coloniai Economic Foundations of the Benin Kingdom ", by P.A. Igbafe, in Topics *on Nigerian Economic and Social History,* {ed} I.A. Akinjogbin and S.O. Osoba, Ife, 1980, page 34.

34. For a detailed account of this see Abubakar, pages 621-24, pages 728-31; and Tukur, pages 29-31.

35. Falola, pages 147-49; and Akintoye, Revolution *and Power Politics,* pages 212-14.

36. The reports of the Political Bureau and of the All-Nigeria Conference on Foreign Policy submitted to the Federal Military Government on Thursday and Friday 26th and 27th March 1987, confirm that this is the direction the majority of Nigerians want for the country, and open a new stage in the struggle for the unity of our country and the dignity and social progress for all its people.

APPENDICES

APPENDIX A: The Abiola-Benson Correspondence*

T.O.S. Benson's Letter:

> Poroye Chambers,
> 119 Broad Street,
> (3rd Floor), Lagos,
> 30th October, 1979.

Dear Alhaji Abiola,

I have just been informed that you have succeeded in excluding me from the proposed ₦18 million sub-contract for prefabricated buildings in connection with Ministry of Communications contract.

I am not at all surprised at your decision, although I had in fact gone into considerable expense in creating facilities for the execution of the contract but what causes me some concern is the reason allegedly given by you. It has in fact come to my knowledge that you have withheld the award of the contract to the Belgium Company because of my association with them and the fact that you do not like my political views and/or current stand.

As you are no doubt aware, I have been in politics since the inception of party politics in Nigeria and over the years, I have been known to express my political views and connections without any fear or favour and without mincing my words. With the current political situation, whilst I might have my reservations as to the conduct of the elections, I have counselled that all the parties should accept the verdict of the

---

*Published, *Sunday Punch*, 11th November, 1979.

court and work towards the stability and unity of the nation. My call for all-party government has-been vindicated by the reported moves of President Shehu Shagari to involve other political parties in his government, which will indeed augur well for the future of this country. There are of course people with vision and patriotism who appreciate that the stability of the nation is more important than quick political gains. I owe no apologies for my declared views and no amount of money can persuade me from expressing my views.

It is with regret therefore, that your decision with regards to the sub-contract was influenced by our political differences. And as if that was not enough, you even threatened my Belgium partners that unless they ceased all business transactions with me, they will be deported as your party is in power. This you will agree with me, is going a little bit too far as you no doubt realise that the country belongs to all of us irrespective of party affiliations. I am definitely sure that President Shehu Shagari, knowing him as I do, will not because of political differences, threaten or attempt to frustrate his political opponents' business endeavours.

I am sure you are aware of my simple character and that it has always been my fervent prayer that people should succeed in their endeavours. Although human memory is short, you will no doubt recall when His Majesty, the Alake of Abeokuta was displeased with you over some matters about five years ago, I called on you in your 4th floor office at 119, Broad Street and advised you as to how to resolve the issue. At first, you proved difficult but eventually you bowed down to the voice of wisdom.

By this your politically motivated and victimised-decision:

1. I have lost over ₦10000 being expenses in travelling to and from Brussels and other incidental expenses.
2. I have been deprived of my share of the project in the ₦18 million sub-contract.
3. I have also lost the partnership of Mr. Yvo Borra as he is scared of having any further dealings with me on account of your injunction.

You can see. Dear Alhaji, the loss you have caused me and if you can victimise a person of my status, only Allah knows what you are capable of doing to people who are not well placed. But let me remind you, that in the words of Psalm 62, Verse II that "Power belongeth to God." And so it is also written in the Koran. It is also pertinent to mention that financial power corrupts just as absolute power corrupts absolutely.

This simple act of yours could have ruined me financially if I had no other means of livelihood and yet you seem to derive some personal satisfaction from this as a Moslem. I am of course aware that you are hardworking and very rich as a gesture of unlimited government patronage. But one thing you have to appreciate is that money is not everything and a Yoruba adage says *"Enfa ju owo to"*. Quite frankly, I owe you no grudge and indeed my prayer is that you may continue to prosper. It is also an adage that *"Qmoaju baba lo"*, and as you are presently in a better financial position than some people of my age group, so also we are financially better off than your father.

I have of course been warned of your ITT political and financial might, and if anything should happen to me, you will be the first to be held responsible.

The above notwithstanding, may I seize this opportunity to wish you and members of your family Barka da Sallah.

With kind regards and Allah's blessing.

Yours faithfully,

CHIEF THEOPHILUS OWOLABI SHOBOWOLE BENSON
(Jagunlabi Ade-Kilumo)

M.K.O.Abiola's Reply;

Ref: MKOA/OMA/CCE.OKP)
8th November, 1979.

My Dear Chief Benson,

Your letter dated 30th October, 1979 was a shocking surprise, waiting for me on arrival from Abeokuta where I celebrated Sallah. I was to have met you to discuss it but learnt you have since travelled out. When I heard you sent copies to several eminent Nigerians without such an indication on my own copy, I feel I should make the whole matter public and let the public judge the issue. Your letter is, therefore, being published side-by-side with this my reply.

The substance of your letter can be summarised as follows:

i.   that I excluded you from the proposed ₦18 million sub-contract for pre-fabricated buildings in connection with the Ministry of Communications contract because of your association with a Belgian Company;

ii.   that the decision in (i) above was also influenced by our political differences;

iii.   that I am very rich as a gesture of my unlimited government patronage;

iv.   that I, though a Muslim, seem to derive some satisfaction to ruin you financially and that if I can victimise a person of your status, only Allah knows what I am capable of doing to people who are not well-placed.

142

You finally ended up by warning that I would be held responsible if anything should happen to you because of my ITT political and financial might.

I reply to the points enumerated above serially in the succeeding paragraphs:

(1) As regards (i) above, I have to state emphatically that I have no knowledge of a "proposed ₦18 million sub-contract" involving you, neither have I threatened any Belgian or any foreigner for that matter, with deportation. On the contrary, the Belgian Embassy will tell you that I am one of the best friends of Belgium in this country. As one who moves around the world, I am always conscious of the need to treat all people of every nationality as well as I would want to be treated.

I have a multi-national team of management personnel, working for and with me in and out of Nigeria without whose support I would never have attained my present position. As for Mr. Y. Borra, your Belgian partner, I wish to assert that "I have not seen him for the past 3 years, neither have I talked to him or anybody else about you since party political activities was lifted in this country. However, I discovered that a company, represented by a Mr. Borra, submitted a quotation to my house in my absence on the 29th October, 1979. In this regard, I attach a photocopy of the Gate Pass completed by him which shows clearly the date and time he came to my house. The envelope contained the proposals from a new company whose address was c/o Belgian Embassy, Lagos. It is also pertinent to mention that "YOUR NAME WAS NOT IN THE LETTER-HEADING EITHER AS A DIRECTOR OR IN ANY CAPACITY WHATSOEVER", and since you have not offered me with a copy of an encyclopedia of "TOS BENSON'S BUSINESS CONTACTS", I find it very difficult to associate you with the proposal submitted by Mr. Borra.

As regards the sub-contract in question, I want to point out that every company we know of in that business was given an opportunity to quote, but we clearly stated that we would prefer those based in Nigeria. It is a matter of policy for companies in which I am associated to deal with indigenous Nigerian enterprises. Besides the fact that Mr. Borra's quotation was addressed c/o Belgian Embassy, Lagos, we had already submitted our recommendation based on quotations submitted by other companies to the Ministry of Communications two days before Mr. Borra turned up in my house. This is a fact you can verify from the Ministry of Communications. Your contention, therefore, that I excluded you from the proposed contract because of your association with a Belgian company is without any foundation.

A man of your experience, who was once a Minister, should know that the mere fact of submission of tender by any firm does not, in any way guarantee an award of contract. Companies with which I am associated with have submitted scores of tenders without a single award of contract since 1976 and we had no cause to shed crocodile tears and impute motives.

(2) With regard to (ii) above, it is far from the truth to say that failure to consider the quotation submitted by your Belgian associate was influenced by our political differences. I can assure you that your political views are yours and have nothing to do with me. I respect them as I have respected the views of everybody else, knowing fully well that human beings are by nature political animals.-It would be a very odd

144

country in which the 80 million people will share the same political views. That being so, I have no cause to bear any grudge against you or any Nigerian for that matter, on political or any ground. I expect people who hold contrary political views to mine to reciprocate this gesture too. I have never seen any basic difference between us in the position you had taken on the major issues confronting this country. Undoubtedly, you must have been grossly misinformed about my opinion about you because I had respect for you as one of the early leaders of this country. Who am I, therefore, to abuse or in any way antagonise you? What shall I gain from taking such a stand? In any case, I am not as foolish as your informants must have painted me!

Contrary to malicious rumours being circulated in some quarters, nobody has been victimised in any of my organisations for his political belief. Partly because we have completed our contracts and have got no new ones since 1976 and partly because profit levels have shrunk considerably, we have had to do away with non-technical staff in administration, personnel, and other clerical functions to keep our head above water. In any case, why all the recent shouts about retrenchment of about 20 staff out of about 3,000 staff by ITT Nigeria Limited when other companies are laying off thousands of staff without any murmur? For every Nigerian staff that was laid off in ITT, ten expatriates have had to go. That is the fact,

(3) As regards (iii) above, it is a matter of public record, which I have asserted on many occasions in public statements without any contradiction, that my business interests in Nigeria have had no major contract award since 1976. This is also a fact. In this connection, am aware that people like you,

who hold different political views from mine, have been making mountains out of mole hills regarding my business ventures.

As far as my business transactions in this country are concerned, all the ills and misfortunes of the Ministry of Communications have been placed on my company by the uninformed and ignorant people like you who are bent on twisting facts for their selfish ends. The companies with which I have been associated have not, under any circumstances, been given any favoured treatment by the government or its agencies. All contracts in which my companies are associated were won strictly on competitive basis. The facts are available for any sensible person to check up.

Contrary to popular conception, ITT or any of the companies associated with me have NOTHING to do 'with laying of cables in Lagos area and digging of Lagos roads.

(4) Regarding (iv) above, I wish to state that if you know anything about what it is to be a Muslim, you will appreciate that Muslims derive no pleasure in ruining their fellowmen as you claimed. I can say, without any fear or favour, that I am not merely a stout Muslim but my life and attitude have been guided by Islamic injunctions. My record in giving assistance to my fellowmen to the best of my ability, compares favourably with that of anybody anywhere. It is a general adage that "the devil will always cite scriptures to suit its purpose". I am not, therefore, surprised by your quotation from Psalm 62.

As a Christian, I would always expect you to bear in mind the Biblical saying which enjoins you not only "to love your neighbours as yourself", but also "to do unto others as you would wish them to do unto you". If you are not prejudiced about my achievements in life, I see no reason why as a good Christian, you should circulate copies of your letter to many eminent Nigerians instead of dropping a line to me as an elderly person, requesting me to see you and iron out some misgivings that were brought to you about the "project". THE LORD SEETH THE MINDS OF ALL OF US AND HE SHALL JUDGE US ACCORDINGLY. JUDGE US BY OUR WORDS AND ACTIONS.

Finally, 1 would like to take this opportunity to reply .to one or two comments or assertions you made in your letter which appear to me to have extended beyond the minor issue of "sub-contract" and your purported expenditure of ₦10,000.

Firstly, it is not true that I "proved difficult" in your discussion with me about His Highness, Kabiyesi, the ALake of Egbaland. You are not an Egba man and the Alake knows that my loyalty to him was never in doubt. Secondly, it is wicked to accuse me of threatening your interests when you never told me, at any time, that such an interest existed, i have never had any business chat with you on this or any other issue since 1974. You did not drop me any note on this "project", so how am I supposed to know your interests were, in it? Sentiments apart, I have no business with you to justify the loud noise you made on this matter. To accuse me of "ruining you financially", is, in the circumstances, false. It is nothing short of blackmail, which is most unexpected from a man about 20 years-older than myself.

In conclusion, I must confess that I was surprised that an experienced Nigerian legal practitioner of your calibre, who has risen to the eminent post of Federal Minister in this country, can jump-into conclusions based on some information given to him by a third party without ascertaining the facts, it is the usual legal parlance that 'hearsay evidence is untenable in law'. If you have checked your facts correctly from me in the first instance, you would have had no cause to resort to the line of action taken by you unless, of course, you have other ulterior motives. The fact that you have circulated the letter to several Nigerians, without giving such indication on my copy, has clearly indicated that you have some malice against me, for reasons best known to you. I put everything before God the Almighty to judge. You have annoyed me, no doubt, deliberately, for reasons best known to you. If all you alleged are in fact the case, God will punish me – there is no way out. If all you wrote are from your wild imagination calculated to tarnish my image, I leave you to God to judge you accordingly.

Unlike you, I do not believe that any human institution, like ITT, can do me any harm, I believe God controls my life and destiny. Here again, you seem to be a victim of your own thinking. If something is wrong with you, I believe you have nobody but God, who must have originated it, to turn to, for solace. That, probably, is one of the basic differences between the two of us. "As you make your bed so you will sleep on it". Up till this moment, I would never have thought that you could fabricate lies against me without any attempt at verification.

May God forgive you, although I doubt from your fetter that you really genuinely believe in Him.

Yours faithfully,
MOSHOOD ABIOLA

APPENDIX B: Our Pact With Awo: Text of a Statement by Dr. Datti Ahmed, Spokesman of the Committee of Concerned Citizens*

Ladies and Gentlemen of the World Press:

Of recent, especially in the last few weeks, there has been intense debate, especially on the radio, on the agreement entered into between Chief Obafemi Awolowo and the Unity Party of Nigeria on the one hand, and the 'Committee of Concerned Citizens', variously called 'the Northern Group', 'the Northern Intellectuals', 'the Mafia', etc.

Intense interest is being shown in the reasons for our entering into this agreement with the Unity Party of Nigeria (UPN) and its Presidential Candidate as well as "in the terms of the agreement as they affect the Northern and predominantly Muslim, part of the country.

The main purpose of this Press Conference is to inform the Nigerian public, especially the voting public, why we entered into the agreement and the terms of the agreement as they affect the Northern part of the country which has, in the past, resisted Chief Obafemi Awolowo's approaches for fear of certain things that are alleged might happen under his leadership of the country, and which this part of the country might not accept. It is to eliminate these fears and re-assure the Northern part of the country in the interests of the unity, peace, stability and prosperity of all the parts of the country that the historic agreement has been entered into by the two sides to the agreement.

---

*Text of Statement by the Committee of Concerned Citizens, *Nigerian Tribune*, Saturday, 6th August, 1983, P-2.

Our reasons for entering into this agreement are as follows:

"After giving very careful consideration to the very disturbing and deteriorating economic and security situation in our country, the 'Committee of Concerned Citizens' felt compelled to search for solutions to these very dangerous economic and security situations before our country slides deeper into those zones of national disaster from which no nation in history has ever found it easy to recover.

Following many meetings of the 'Committee of Concerned Citizens' during the early months of this year, the committee became convinced that these twin ills of economic disaster and frightening security situation are the results of, in particular, poor and ineffective government at the centre. The committee was further convinced that no improvement can be expected towards the provision of good government, as presently constituted and led. The committee was, therefore, convinced that the only way to avert the impending national disaster is to work towards the democratic installation of a more patriotic, humane, purposeful and competent Federal Government to replace the present one after the 1983 National Elections.

The aims of the Committee of Concerned Citizens are:

1. To help to install a democratic Federal Government that will enjoy country-wide support through widely spread participation and thus enable the government to enjoy stability so that the country may enjoy peace,

progress and security of lives, property and employment.

2. To arrest and then reverse the avoidable severe economic recession our country is passing through, and which has resulted in the loss of hundreds of jobs with resulting untold suffering, hardship and humiliation of those who have lost employment, and their dependents.

3. To revamp the nation's economy so that the crip-pung shortages of everything, from raw materials for our industries to spare parts for our vital establishments such as the NEPA, P & T, our various water works, our factories and down to such basic essential consumer goods such as soaps and detergents for personal and domestic uses, may be arrested and so that these absolutely essential commodities may begin to be brought into the country before irreparable damages are done to these vital institutions in the country.

4. To reverse the state of insecurity which causes the majority of the citizens to live in fear of their lives and properties from the menace of armed robbers and other law breakers who seem to prosper and proliferate to the great shock and frustration of the vast majority of the law-abiding and peace-loving citizens of the country.

5. To put a stop to the shameful and ostentatious corruption being perpetrated against the country and its citizens by the few privileged, but unpatriotic, greedy and inhumane men who have found themselves in positions of trust and authority and have betrayed the trust and perverted the authority to their own narrow

selfish ends, to the great suffering of the vast majority of the peace-loving and law-abiding citizens of the country.

Towards this end, the Committee of Concerned Citizens has examined very critically the available democratic choices before it and has resolved to support whomsoever amongst the six contesting Presidential Candidates, appears to the committee to be the one likely to provide the type of Federal Government the committee has pledged itself, as described above, to help, to install in the country after the 1983 National Elections. In pursuance of this, the committee carried out very critical examination of the merits of each of the six Presidential Candidates and their respective political parties, for the purpose of selecting the one candidate who is most likely to be able to translate the aims and objectives of the committee into realities should he and his party win the forthcoming presidential elections. As a result of this critical examination the committee unanimously agreed that Chief Obafemi Awolowo and the Unity Party of Nigeria are the obvious choice.

Following the decision of the committee on the suitability of Chief Obafemi Awolowo and the Unity Party of Nigeria, the committee again unanimously agreed to accept their long standing invitation to the committee to enter into dialogue with him and his party for the purpose of working together towards success in the 1983 elections.

Arising from this mutual agreement between Chief Awolowo and the Unity Party of Nigeria on the one hand and the Committee of Concerned Citizens on the other, each side appointed a high-powered delegation to a conference of the two sides. The two delegations met on several occasions and finally worked out the terms that will govern this historic co-operation, the great benefits of which to the country in terms of peace, stability and progress for all sections of the country only the future can fully reveal.

The terms of this Cooperation Agreement are as follows:

1. That the committee shall provide a respectable and acceptable Presidential running mate to Chief Awolowo.

2. That the committee will use every democratic means at their disposal to mobilise support for the Unity Party of Nigeria's Presidential ticket with the clear objective of securing at least 25 per cent of the votes cast in the Presidential elections in each of the ten Northern States.

3. That the committee shall organise respectable candidates with good prospects to contest for the gubernatorial offices in the Northern States.

4. That the committee shall organise candidates with good prospects to contest the seats in both the National and State Assemblies in all the ten Northern States.

5. On the party winning the Presidential election, the committee shall recommend the best, available men from the Northern States to participate in running the Federal Government and its Agencies so that the country may experience good and stable government and by far the best the country has ever known.

The Unity Party of Nigeria and its Presidential Candidate, Chief Obafemi Awolowo, covenant with the Committee of Concerned Citizens that if Chief Awowolo wins the elections and becomes President of the Federal Republic of

Nigeria, he shall carry out the following undertakings given by him and the Unity Party of Nigeria to the Committee of Concerned Citizens:

1. *Education*

That his Federal Government shall institute and carry out an effective programme of bridging the educational gap between the educationally advantaged States and the educationally disadvantaged States in the North especially investing in infra-structural facilities in the latter States so that they too may benefit meaningfully from the free education policy of the party.

Islamic Religious and Moral Education: That the Federal Government shall actively encourage and financially support the teaching of Islamic Religious knowledge and morals in all educational institutions attended by Muslims.

2. *HAJJ by Muslims*

The Federal Government shall allow every Muslim who desires and has the means to perform the Hajj during any year of his choice and the new government shall immediately do away with the Shagari-imposed restriction on the number of Muslim pilgrims to the Holy Land of Saudi Arabia.

3. *Agriculture*

The Federal Government shall continue to actively pursue the development of the River Basin Authorities as a major part of its integrated rural development programme with the view to providing meaningful farming occupations to the rural farmers in the North in particular and also to make the country self-sufficient in food.

4. *Foreign Policy.*

The Federal Government will maintain friendly relations with all countries. The establishment of embassies and the maintenance of such embassies will be determined by the highest interest of the Nigerian nation. Where diplomatic relations have been broken by the previous administration, the Federal Government will review each case on its merit. In the case of Israel, the review of the diplomatic relationship of Nigeria with that country will not be automatic.

The view of all parts of the country and the overriding interest of the Nigerian nation, will be taken into consideration if and when such a review is considered necessary.

5. *Ethical Banking Acceptable to Islam*

The Federal Government will permit the establishment of banking institutions which on ethical grounds, may not charge interest but may operate on the basis of the bank holding shares in the business of the borrower and sharing in the profits or losses of the business.

6. *Abuja as the Capital Territory*

That the Federal Government will actively continue with the development of the new Federal Capital at Abuja and will ensure the movement of the seat of the Federal Government to the capital within the shortest possible time.

7. *Distribution of Political Offices*

That the President shall appoint people from the North into key positions and Ministries so that the participation of the Northern part of the country will be seen in the North as obvious and important. The President shall consult the Committee of Concerned Citizens in respect of such offices that should be occupied by Northern States appointees.

Notes

1. According to Ebenezer Babatope this was what happened: "Many meetings were held between this group (led by Dr. Datti Ahmed, a private medical practitioner in Kano) and the UPN. The UPN delegation to the meeting was led by Alhaji Lateef Kayode Jakande. I was also a member of the delegation, as the then Director of Organisation of the UPN. The 'Committee of Concerned Citizens' which allegedly enjoyed the support of Major General Shehu Yar'Adua, Chief of Staff Supreme Headquarters in General Olusegun Obasanjo's administration entered into an Alliance with the UPN because of its belief that the NPN was slowly destroying the unity and peace of the country. The spokesman of the group was Dr. Mahmud Tukur who later became the Minister of Commerce and Industry in General Buhari's administration. . .. Other members of the group were Dr. Suleman Kumo and Alhaji Yahaya Abubakar, a retired federal permanent secretary and Chairman of the Federal Radio Corporation under Buhari's administration. The group was believed to be the principal instigators of 31st December 1983 coup. Throughout our meetings with them they showed a clear understanding of the problems facing Nigeria and they were quite eager to participate in their solutions. I was later informed in prison that these men of the Committee of Concerned Citizens had merely deceived the UPN by signing an electoral Alliance with the party. I am unable to

corroborate this allegation because my imprisonment did not allow me to observe the group from very close quarters." From E. Babatope's *Murtala Muhammed: A Leader Betrayed (A Study in Buhari's Tyranny)*, Roy and Ezete Publishing Co. Ltd., Enugu, 1986, pp. 83-84.

APPENDIX C: Nigerian Foreign Policy Should Actively Foster Nigerian Unity Based on Our African Identity and Destiny*

1.   We, the undersigned citizens of the Federal Republic of Nigeria, who have no other country in the world but this one, note with deep concern the way antagonism between Nigerians belonging to different religious faiths is being deliberately encouraged, over the issues of Nigeria's relationship with Israel, with the Organisation of Islamic Conference and the Vatican. This campaign of systematic manipulation of religious sentiments, is being conducted for the sinister and reactionary purpose of diverting the attention of the people of this country from the urgent tasks of economic reconstruction and the working out of a new political order in which we can forge our unity, develop our country, and achieve social justice, political stability and genuine national independence. In the long term, the purpose of this campaign of political manipulation of religious sentiments, is to entrench religious conflicts in all facets of our National life, so that the Nigerian agents of imperialism, working under the cover of Christianity and Islam, financed by Zionism and Arab reaction, can always hold the unity of this country at ransom, build up the   forces   for   its destruction, and ultimately break it up, so as to give a serious blow to the movements for democracy, social and national liberation, which are now making great advances all over the African continent.

---

*Published in *The Triumph*, 29th January, 1986; *The Nigerian Standard* 31st January, 1986; *New Nigerian*, 3rd February, 1986; 3rd February, 1986.

2. The individuals, groups, and organisations waging This campaign against the unity of the people of this country, are particularly afraid of, and very hostile, to popular mobilisation and debate at the grass-roots level over who, and what, is responsible for what has gone wrong in this country in the last twenty-five years, and how these retrograde and backward forces and elements can be overcome for genuine economic, social and political progress. They therefore wear the Cloak Of religion in order to confuse and divert the attention of our people from their harsh conditions of existence, and how to positively transform these conditions in a permanent and systematic fashion.

3. We are particularly concerned that the Federal Military Government in its role in this matter has not clearly identified and pursued the real interests of the people of Nigeria.

4. There is no doubt about the seriousness of the faith and the commitment of most Nigerians in their religious beliefs. There is also no doubt that Islam and Christianity contain fundamental moral principles on which aspects of our society and culture are built. There is no doubt about the richness, and breadth, of the cultural heritage our people find in religion and in its significant role in their historical experience. Of all these there can be no doubt whatsoever. The development of the people of Nigeria cannot therefore be separated from their religious beliefs.

5. But, there is a world of difference between the fundamental moral and ethical principles of human equality, human dignity, democracy and social justice at the foundation of both Christianity and Islam, and the way religious rhetoric, religious affiliation, and religious symbolism are used to promote, and protect, the various systems of human

oppression, human degradation and exploitation operating all over our country today. There is a world of difference between the messages of hope, harmony and justice which Jesus Christ and the Prophet Muhammed (SAW) brought to humanity, and the sinister, oppressive, divisive, corrupt preaching activities and the day to day activities of most of the leading contemporary Nigerian *ulema*, clerics, *khadis*, bishops and all those rich and powerful parasites hiding behind a show of religious piety in this country today. When these people deal with the legal system in this country, it is not, how to protect the rights of the peasant farmer to his farmland; the orphan to his inheritance; the mother to her children; the worker to the products of his labour; or the citizen to the resources of his country, which they address themselves to. When they deal with the crisis of education in this country, it is not how to provide education for all the children and adults of Nigeria so as to develop their mental and manual creativity, and sense of personal dignity and national consciousness, which they address themselves to. Over these and all other issues dealing with the welfare of the people and the progress of society, their concern is how to promote their high status, power, large incomes and how to perpetuate these as the gatemen between their communities and the rest of the country, and the world. The type of religion represented by these types of clerics and their lay patrons and masters cannot be used to promote the national interests of Nigeria, because it is fundamentally opposed to these interests and serves foreign and domestic interests directly opposed and hostile to these.

6. These hard facts about the nature and role of religion in Nigeria have to be seen in the context of the composition,

position and location of Nigeria in the world today. We are the largest nation-state on the African continent in terms of population, God, in His infinite wisdom, has endowed us with massive human and material resources. But like other Africans, and black men and women everywhere in the world, we have for over four hundred years been enslaved, exploited, oppressed and massacred. Our people have had their differences of religion, language, culture and territory turned into violent divisions which are used to set them against one another to facilitate the enslavement and exploitation of one another and often to massacre each other. It is less than twenty years ago when between 1966 and 1970, our own country went through a tragic experience in which differences over religion, and territory were manipulated by our domestic and foreign exploiters to throw us at each other's throat.

7.   What all this means is that a fundamental and supreme objective of our domestic as well as foreign policies, has to be, the forging of our national unity, which includes the refusal to allow anyone to use our differences in religion, language, culture and territory to divide us. Since our experience has shown us that religion is one element which has been manipulated and is being manipulated today to undermine our unity, weaken and block our attempts at achieving our national independence, we have to establish as a major pillar of our foreign policy the principle that our country shall never join any international religious organisation as a nation-state. We shall also not get involved at the level of our diplomatic relations with any such organisation. In consistence with this principle, based on the recognition of the facts set out above, the following actions and

commitments should right now be made by the Federal Military Government:

i. The affirmation of the principle that a fundamental objective of Nigeria foreign policy is to promote the unity of Nigeria based on its African identity and destiny and in recognition of this and its history and role in the African continent and the world, she shall not join any international organisation based on religious solidarity or have diplomatic relations with any international religious institution;

ii. In keeping with this principle, the Federal Military Government should immediately and categorically, terminate all diplomatic relations with any international religious institution, and any membership in any international religious organisation, like the Organisation of Islamic Conference, which have already been entered into or are in the process of being entered into;

iii. The recognition that individual Nigerian citizens can in the exercise of their fundamental human rights of association belong to an organisation which affiliates with international religious organisations and institutions, as long as this affiliation is not used to undermine the unity of the country;

iv. The affirmation of the principle that Nigeria, consistent with its role and history shall not have any diplomatic relationship with any state built upon racial segregation, like the apartheid state of South Africa and the Zionist state of Israel, in each of which one has to either belong to the white race in the former or the Jewish race in the latter, before one can be a citizen;

v. Consistent with our destiny, role and responsibility in the world, the Federal Military Government should give full diplomatic status to the representatives of the National Congress of South Africa (A.N.C.) and the South West African Peoples Organisation (S.W.A.P.O.) and follow these up with commensurate and sustained military assistance, to further affirm our uncompromising commitment to our African identity, destiny and to the total liberation of the African continent.

8. We, the undersigned, like 99.% of the people of this country have no other country but this one. We have no houses, bank accounts, other assets, connections or patrons and protectors anywhere in the world. Nigeria is the only place on God's earth we belong to. We shall therefore do anything to promote and defend its unity and interests. Long live the Federal Republic of Nigeria.

(Signed by:)
Abdullahi Mahadi
George Kwanashie
Yusufu Bala Usman
Eli Jiddere Bala
Musa Audu
Monday Mangvwat
Alkasum Abba
Wilberforce Hinjari

Ahmadu Bello University, Zaria,
27th January, 1986.

APPENDIX D: The Violent Politics of Religion and the Survival of Nigeria*

Since last Friday, 6th March, 1987, violent attacks have been launched against life, property and places of worship in most of the major cities and towns of Kaduna State. Churches and Mosques; hotels and cinemas; businesses and vehicles; private homes and persons have been attacked, smashed up and systematically set on fire, in an unprecedented campaign of violent religious politics clearly aimed against the survival of our country.

In these seven days many people have been killed and wounded. Many more have been harassed, molested, completely frightened and made totally insecure. Over a hundred Churches and a few Mosques have been burnt down completely. Right now in Zaria, almost all economic, educational and other activities have stopped. Hundreds of people are on the roads, the motor parks and railway stations looking for transport to travel back to their hometowns for safety and security. The basis of normal life has been severely shaken. In spite of reports and warnings from concerned individuals and organisations, three days after the start of the violence, Police and Security forces were completely absent from the scenes. Citizens were left completely at the mercy of the violent mobs. This apparent abdication of responsibility by Government must be taken very seriously. This type of violent campaign of Muslims against Christians is unprecedented in the history of our country. It directly threatens her continued survival as a single entity.

"Published in *New Nigerian*, 20th March, 1987, and *The Guardian*, 25th March, 1937.

We, the undersigned citizens of the Federal Republic of Nigeria, who have no other country in the world but this one, have witnessed and personally experienced this violent attack against one of the foundations on which our country exists, namely the *secular nature of the Nigerian State* and its duty to protect the rights of everyone to practice his/her own religion without any hindrance whatsoever.

In January 1986, some of us were forced to issue a signed statement warning over the way Nigeria's relations with the Organisation of Islamic Conference, Israel and the Vatican were being used by sinister and reactionary forces to undermine the unity of our people and the sovereignty and integrity of our nation. In that statement titled *Nigerian Foreign Policy Should Actively Foster Nigerian Unity Based on Our African Identity and Destiny*, it was pointed out that "this campaign of systematic manipulation of religious sentiments is being conducted for the sinister and reactionary purpose of diverting the attention of the people of this country from the urgent tasks of economic reconstruction and the working out of a new political order in which we can forge our unity, develop our country, and achieve social justice, political stability and genuine national independence. In the long term, the purpose of this campaign of political manipulation of religious sentiments is to entrench religious conflicts in all facets of our national life, so that the Nigerian agents of imperialism, working under the cover of Christianity and Islam, financed by Zionism and Arab reaction, can always hold the unity of this country to ransom, build up the forces for its destruction, and ultimately break it up so as to give a serious blow to the movements for democracy, social and national liberation, which are now making great advances all over Africa. The individuals, groups and organisations waging this campaign against the unity of the people of this country, are particularly afraid of, and very hostile, to popular mobilisation and debate at the grassroots level over who, and what, is responsible for what has gone wrong with this country in the last twenty-five years, and how these retrograde and backward forces and elements can be overcome for genuine economic, social and political progress. They therefore wear the cloak of religion in order to confuse and divert the attention of our people from their harsh conditions of existence, and how to positively transform these conditions in a permanent and systematic fashion."

Our experience of the current events and all the evidence available to us, have convinced us that the violence and arson of the last seven days was not the brain work of the hooligans. It is, however, believed to be the latest stage of a campaign which started about ten years ago, in the so-called 'Shari'a Debate', in the Constituent Assembly in 1976/77. At that time it was aimed at creating political constituencies for political leaderships, whose records showed that they had nothing to offer our people. This strategy failed and therefore they now turn again to the manipulation of religious sentiments and religious symbols to cover up their complete bankruptcy and failures.

Right now we can see behind the killing, maiming and arson, a return to the 1976/77 scenario. Only this time the level of violence and the threat to national security and survival is much higher. But just as 1976/77 was only two to three years away from a return to civilian democracy, so 1986/87 is also only two to three years away from a return to civilian democracy in 1990. The basic difference, however, is that progressive developments among the people of Nigeria, and the rest of Africa, over the last ten years have made these backward and reactionary forces more determined to entrench religious conflict in Nigeria, paralyse it in internecine and bloody conflicts like the Lebanon and the Sudan, and to ultimately wreck it, when appropriate.

We are convinced that this campaign has reached this-totally unacceptable and very dangerous level because successive Federal Governments have toyed with one of the foundations on which Nigerian unity exists, namely the secular nature of the Nigerian State and its sacred responsibility to protect the right of belief and worship of everyone.

A strong impression has been created that some organisations and individuals can, with arrogance and impunity, incite and threaten people of other religious beliefs and will get away with, at most, only verbal reprimands or appeals to be tolerant.

We are convinced that this campaign of violent religious politics has reached the very dangerous levels it has because several powerful media organs, particularly the Federal Radio Corporation of Nigeria, Kaduna, have been allowed to be used by a tiny backward oligarchy which survives on inciting one section of Nigeria against another. Anybody who listens to the English and particularly the Hausa programmes of the Federal Radio Corporation of Nigeria, Kaduna since January 1986, and particularly since Monday 9th March, 1987, knows that something sinister and violent was being systematically planned against the unity of the people of Nigeria, and against the peace and stability in the country.

We the undersigned therefore want to warn, in a very solemn way, all our brothers and sisters in this country, that we are fast coming to the brink of catastrophe. The events of the last seven days are very serious and very dangerous for our individual and collective survival. All those citizens committed to the unity of this country, for which so much blood has been shed, have to stand up and make a choice between fear, timidity, and inertia in the face of systematic destruction of the foundation of our nation, and a determined struggle to crush these forces of destruction and save our country and our future.

We call on the Federal Military Government to shed all ambiguities and hesitation, and to declare and reaffirm that the Nigerian State is SECULAR and one of its most fundamental responsibilities is to *protect the right of every citizen and resident to practice the religion of their choice* We call on the Federal Military Government to implement this decisively and clearly in practice by identifying publicly, and punishing according to the taw, all the rich and powerful individuals who are known to be behind this campaign of violent religious politics aimed at destroying our country.

We call on the Federal Military Government to ensure in all parts of the country, the security of life and property and of places and of freedom of belief and worship of every-one.

We call on the Federal Military Government to affirm and promote the exercise of the fundamental human rights of individuals and the collective self-defence of alt the people against any form of aggression, be it external or internal.

We call on the Federal Military Government to make, as a matter of utmost urgency, full reparations to all those

168

who have suffered damages in the events of the past week. In particular, we ask that government ensures that the right to facilities for worship by all religious groups is restored and guaranteed in all places where they have been destroyed. We are convinced that the sinister and utterly reactionary forces behind this campaign of violent religious politics with the aim of destroying our country are made up of a tiny oligarchy determined to maintain its power, wealth and privileges at all costs including violent and well-organised mobs in the name of religion. We are also convinced that the majority of the people of this country and the popular organisations are capable of being mobilised to overcome them and defend the unity of our people and the integrity of our country. We therefore call upon the Nigerian Labour Congress to mobilise all the workers of this country around *a* campaign against religious and all sectional politics.

Long live the Federal Republic of Nigeria.

(Signed by:)
Kyari Tijjani
Paul Izah
Charles Gonyok
Sanusi Abubakar
Yusufu Bala Usman
Zuwaqhu A. Bonat
Yahaya Abdullahi
Monday Mangvwat
Eli Jiddere Bala
Wilberforce Hinjari
Alkasum Abba
Emmanuel Odumuh
George Kwanashie

Mikailu Gutip
Sa'idu Shehu Awak
Stephen Nkom
Saidu Adamu
Ayo Ajagun
Grace Ajagun (Mrs.)
Ahmed Modibbo Mohammed
Abubakar Siddique Mohammed
Oga Ajene

Ahmadu Bello University, Zaria,
13th March, 1987.

THE AUTHOR

Yusufu Bala Usman was born at Musawa, Katsina, Nigeria, in 1945. He now works in the Department of History, Ahmadu Bello University, Zaria.

He is the author of *For the Liberation of Nigeria* (New Beacon Books, London, 1979); *The Transformation of Katsina, 1400-1883: The Emergence and Overthrow of the Sarauta System and the Establishment of the Emirate* (A.B.U. Press, Zaria, 1981); *Nigeria Against the I.M.F.: The Home Market Strategy* (Vanguard, Kaduna, 1986); and is one of the authors of *The Nigerian Economic Crisis: Causes and Solutions* (ASUU, Zaria, 1985): and of various articles in newspapers and journals.

He has edited *Studies in the History of the Sokoto Caliphate,* (Third Press International, New York, 1979), and co-edited with Abdullahi Augie, *Cities of the Savannah* (Nigeria Magazine, Lagos, 1979); with Nur Alkali, *Studies in the History of Pre-Colonial Borno* (N.N.P.C., Zaria, 1983); and with Femi Kayode, *The Economic and Social Development of Nigeria* (Panel on Nigeria Since Independence, Ibadan, 1986).

While he was the Director of Research of the People's Redemption Party, he edited *Tarihin Gwagwarmayar N.E.P.U. da P.R.P.* (The History of the Struggles of the N.E.P.U. and the P.R.P.), written by Mallam Lawan Danbazau (Zaria, 1981); *Who is Responsible? The Nigerian Workers and the Current Economic Crisis* (Zaria, 1982); *Political Repression in Nigeria, 1979-1981: A Selection of Documents: I,* (Zaria, 1982).

Yusufu Bala Usman has been a member of the Committee for the Review of Nigerian Foreign Policy, October 1975-May 1976; of the Constitution Drafting Committee; of the Nigerian Delegation to the People's

Republic of Angola, January 1976; was also a Special Adviser to the Nigerian Delegation to the 31st and 41st Sessions of the U.N. General Assembly, in November 1976, and November 1986; a Trustee of the Nigerian Labour Congress, 1978-80; Co-ordinator of the Transition Programme and Secretary of the Kaduna State Government, 1979-82; member of the Awoniyi Judicial Commission of Inquiry into Contract Awards in Niger State, in April-November 1984; Chairman of the Political Committee of the All-Nigeria Conference on Foreign Policy, Kuru, April 1986; and is a member of *The Analyst* magazine collective. He is married with six children.